Fishing Essentials

FOR
DUMMIES®

by Peter Kaminsky

COURAGE BOOKS
AN IMPRINT OF RUNNING PRESS
PHILADELPHIA • LONDON

© Photodisc pages: 17, 27, 92, 119, 128
© Stockbyte pages: 8, 36, 58, 68, 80, 93, 108
© Corbis pages: 3
© 2001 David R. Prince pages: 6, 7, 32, 40, 45, 49, 56, 60, 67, 76, 87, 96, 99, 105, 106, 115, 116, 122, 127
Front Cover Photos / © 2001 David R. Prince, © Corbis
Back Cover Photos / © Photo Disc

9   8   7   6   5   4   3   2
Digit on the right indicates the number of this printing

Library of Congress Cataloging-in-Publication Number 2001094403
ISBN 0-7624-1265-8

Designed by Matthew W. Goodman
Edited by Michael Washburn
Typography: Cheltenham, Univers and Cascade Script

This book may be ordered by mail from the publisher. Please include $2.50 for postage and handling.
But try your bookstore first!

Published by Courage Books, an imprint of
Running Press Book Publishers
125 South Twenty-second Street
Philadelphia, Pennsylvania 19103-4399

Visit us on the web!
www.runningpress.com

Icons used in this book

With more and more people pressuring fewer and fewer fish, we all need to learn some basic rules of the road.

Having the right fly, lure, rod, hat, shoes, and so on can make all the difference between success and a miserable day. This icon flags the stuff you *really* need.

From a hook in your finger to a dip in a stream, text next to this icon will show you how to stay dry, comfortable, and safe.

This icon flags information that will save you from making the same mistakes that took the rest of us years to unlearn.

Table of Contents

· ·

Chapter 1

Freshwater Fish

In This Chapter

▸ Discovering why rainbows and brookies aren't trout (and why it doesn't matter)

▸ Calming a squirming bass

▸ Revealing the most popular freshwater fish

▸ Picking up a pike without losing one or more fingers

Trout

If the number of words written about a fish is any indication of popularity, then the trouts are the runaway winners. A great deal of what has been written about trout is just a bunch of hot air, but (separating the fish from a bunch of gasbag fishing writers) it is a supreme game fish that is at least the equal of any other sport fish. In the old days, an angler was judged by how many trout he or she brought home; but these days, thanks largely to the influence of American anglers, catch-and-release is more the rule. If you kill the occasional trout, however, don't let anyone make you feel guilty about it. They are delicious fish. On the other hand, if you kill every trout that you catch, you are being more greedy than wise. Trout are the top predator in their environment: They stand at the top of the food chain in many rivers and streams. Top predators are, of necessity, rarer than animals lower down the chain. A little bit of pressure can alter the quality of angling in a stream very quickly. So enjoy yourself, enjoy your meal, but remember that the fish you return to the stream will grow larger and have babies.

Figure 1-1

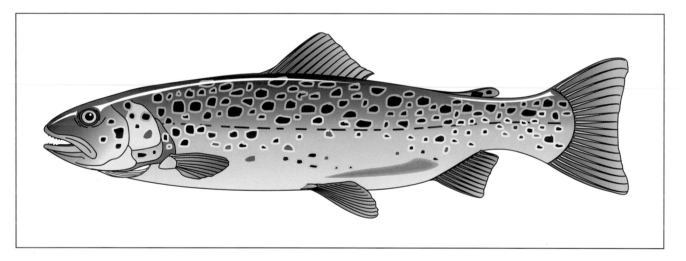

The champ: Brown trout

The brown trout is a fish designed for the angler. It often feeds on the surface. It rises to a properly presented fly. It fights like the dickens. The brown didn't acquire a reputation as a "gentleman's fish" because it had particularly good manners and went to the right school. The simple fact of the matter is that rich English gentlemen, with time on their hands, embraced the sport of angling and popularized it everywhere. Because their local fish was the brown trout, it became the fish of choice for sportsmen there and in the New World. If the English sportsmen had started out in Georgia instead of England, the largemouth bass would probably have a lot of flowery literature. If those same anglers had lived in Mississippi, the local Izaak Walton may well have written about the simple virtues and great sporting qualities of the catfish.

The brown trout is a cold-water fish that lives in lakes and streams and is most active when the water temperature is in the 60s. A temperature much above 80°F is liable to kill brown trout. As shown in Figure 1-1, the brown trout is covered with spots everywhere but its tail. The majority of the spots are deep brown, like coffee beans, with a light yellow halo. Sprinkled around its skin, you also find a few red and yellow spots.

The world record brown trout at 40 pounds, 4 ounces was taken by Howard L. "Rip" Collins on the Little Red River in Heber Springs, Arkansas, on May 9, 1992. (Thanks to the IGFA, which maintains an up-to-date archive of world records.)

Not quite cricket, but so what?

Brown trout are very wary, and they are also creatures of habit. If you know their habits, and the habits of the anglers who fish for them, you may have an advantage that you can exploit. Case in point: my first visit to the Test, one of the historic English trout streams. I visited during the time of year when a large fly, which the English call The Mayfly, hatches. Whereas Americans called all the up-winged aquatic insects mayflies, the English reserve it for this humongous hatch. It is a big fly and makes a fat target. Trout are supposed to be so easy to catch when this hatch is on, English anglers call this time of year "Duffers Fortnight" because, during that hatching period, anybody can catch a trout.

"Anybody" didn't include me. Three or four hours of casting had not yielded even one rise. On a hunch, I cut off my dry fly and tied on a little nymph. I walked upstream and crossed over an old wooden bridge. I walked downstream through thick undergrowth on the unfished side of the river. (With the angler facing upstream, most English trout streams have the left bank cleared so that a right-handed caster can present a fly upstream without hanging up the backcast in pesky branches and grass.) I cast my little nymph about six feet into the current, which was as long a cast as I could manage in those close quarters. I let the fly swing into the bank, and a trout took on my first cast. After an hellacious fight, I landed him. He weighed 61/4 pounds and was the big trout of the season on that river.

To catch him, all I had done was present a fly in a novel way. By using the least-favored bank and breaking the English gentlemen's code that requires an angler to cast upstream only, I proved that although the trout of the Test may have been well educated when it came to mayfly imitations presented by a right-handed caster on the left bank, anything that looked like food and that came from a different direction had a much better chance of interesting a good fish.

The moral of the story is this: Try something different if you have a feeling that it may work. (No law says that you have to fish the way that everybody else does.)

Brown trout are long-lived animals and can reach weights up to 40 pounds, but most stream-bred fish average less than a pound each. They say that a few wise browns in every stream usually reach weights of 10 pounds or more. I've never caught one.

Figure 1-2

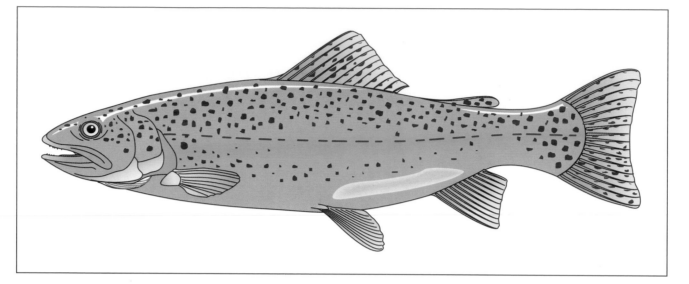

High jumpers: Rainbow trout

Guess what? A couple of years ago, scientists decided that the rainbow trout (see Figure 1-2) isn't a trout after all. This fish looks like a trout and behaves like a trout. It feeds like a trout and eats flies like a trout. Probably because of those characteristics, those same Englishmen who gave us the lore of the brown trout decided to call the rainbow a trout. (Whenever the English arrived in a new country, they gave the local fish and game the names of similar animals back in Merrie Olde England.)

On June 22, 1970, the world record rainbow was caught by David Robert White at Bell Island, Alaska. It weighed 42 pounds and 2 ounces.

Steelhead — a salty rainbow

Almost all species of trout, if given the chance, drop downstream to the ocean where they usually grow to much greater size then trout that are confined to streams and lakes. Sea-run brookies and browns (those that forage in the ocean and return to spawn in fresh water) also appear in North America, but the main target for anglers of sea-run trout is the steelhead, which is nothing more than a rainbow that has gone to sea. Steelhead have usually lost the distinctive coloration of the freshwater rainbow (although they still have the pink lateral line). As their name suggests, steelheads have a bright, metallic coloration.

Figure 1-3

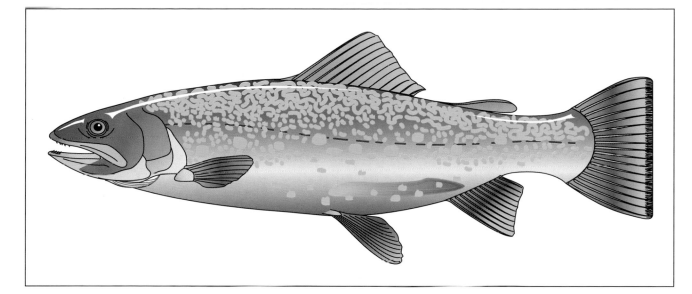

Sentimental favorites: Brookies

Like the rainbow, the brook trout, or *brookie*, isn't a trout. It is the animal that fills the trout niche in the cooler streams of the northeastern U.S., east of the Allegheny Mountains. The brook trout is actually a char, which makes it a relative of the lake trout (not a real trout either), the Dolly Varden, and the Arctic char.

I think that because the *brookie* is found only in wilderness areas explains part of the fondness that anglers have for him. He is a sign of pure water and a healthy ecology. Brookies like cooler water and cannot stand the higher temperatures that the brown and the rainbow can tolerate. Before Europeans cleared the great hardwood forests of the northeastern U.S., most streams had the shade and pure water that brook trout need.

With the clearing of the forests and the coming of brown trout and rainbow trout, the brookie often retreated to the less-accessible headwaters of many streams. As explained by the principle of "smaller fish in smaller water," many people, whose only brook trout experience is on these smaller waters, have assumed that the brook trout is typically smaller than the rainbow or the brown. This is not true. In the old days on Long Island, for example, many brook trout ranged from 4 pounds to 10 pounds.

Although it is much praised for its great beauty, many anglers regard the brookie as an empty-headed glamour-puss. I have to say that I agree in most cases. This isn't to say that very wary, hard-to-catch brookies aren't out there, but by and large, most of them are prettier than they are smart.

The brook trout has many red spots that are surrounded by a blue halo. The fins have a telltale black and white tip. The belly and fins have an orange cast that can be quite brilliant and almost crimson in spawning season. The tail of the brook trout is more squared off than that of the brown and rainbow, hence the nickname *squaretail*.

The world record brook trout (a 14-pound, 8-ounce fish) was caught by Dr. W. J. Cook in the Nipigon River, Ontario, Canada, on July 8, 1916. Before that, the record fish was attributed to none other than Daniel Webster, the great United States senator who is widely thought of as the greatest orator in the history of the United States. Daniel Webster's fish story is a great one, and I have gone through local church records and ancient sporting magazines trying to get some hard evidence of its basis in fact. I never did find any, but it still makes a nice tale.

Figure 1-4

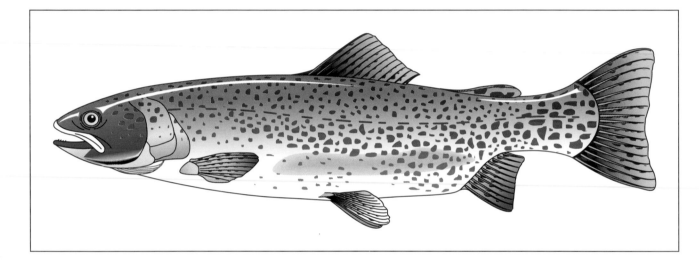

The cutthroat

You may think of the cutthroat — which is really a cousin to the rainbow — as the Rocky Mountain version of the brook trout (shown in Figure 1-3) because in many undisturbed waters, just like the brookie, the cutthroat is the native fish. After ranching, logging, and the introduction of other game fish takes place, the cutthroat often retreats to unpressured headwaters. As with the brook trout, the cutthroat has the reputation of having less intelligence than the brown trout. Apart from the fact that I don't know how one can administer an intelligence test to a brown or a cutthroat, I don't agree. Cutthroats (sometimes called cuts) can be extremely selective. They do not have the bulldog, head-shaking determination of the brown nor the leaping instinct of the rainbow, but in all of Troutdom, there is nothing like the surface take of the cutthroat: He comes up, sips the fly, and shows you his whole body before descending with the fly. All you need to do is come tight to the fish and you're on.

The cutthroat is the native trout in the drainage of the Yellowstone River, where it is protected by a complete no-kill policy in all of the flowing water in Yellowstone Park. To fish them at the outlet of Yellowstone Lake is one of the great angling experiences in North America.

As you can't really see in Figure 1-4, cuts get their name from the slash of red or orange on the jaw and gills. The world record, a 41-pound behemoth, was taken at Pyramid Lake, Nevada, in December 1925, by John Skimmerhor.

Figure 1-5

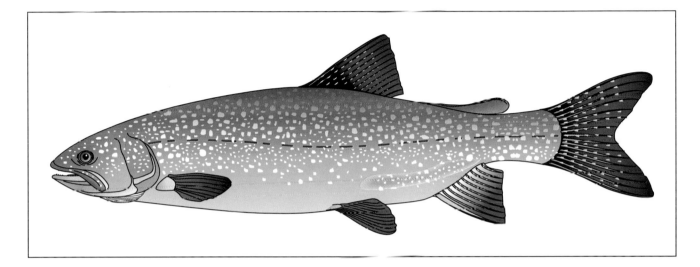

Lakers: Big macks

Widely known as Mackinaws or gray trout, the lake trout (or laker) is the largest char. The Mackinaw requires colder water than any other freshwater game fish, optimally about 50°F, and it will die at 65°F.

Right after ice-out in the spring and right before spawning in the autumn, lakers may be taken in shallow water. But during the rest of the season, anglers have to fish deeper, often trolling with wire line or lead core.

Unlike all the other trout (true trout as well as rainbows and chars), the laker spawns in lakes, not streams. This fact is much on the minds of biologists in Yellowstone Park, where some lame-brains dumped a few lakers in Yellowstone Lake a few years ago. Prior to that, this lake held the last pure strain of cutthroats in the Rockies. The lakers began to prey on young cutthroat fry. This situation was bad enough. But because lakers don't run up the rivers as the cuts do, about 20 percent of the food supply of the grizzly bear, osprey, and eagle have been removed from the ecosystem. This is a prime case of messing with Mother Nature. I don't blame the fish, however. In fact, I like lakers. I do blame the fishermen who dumped the lakers in Yellowstone Lake, though.

As shown in Figure 1-5, the laker, like the brookie, is heavily spotted. It has a forked tail (in contrast to the square tail of the brookie). The largest one ever taken on rod and reel weighed 66 pounds and 8 ounces and was caught in Canada's Great Bear Lake on July 10, 1991. A 102-pound laker was netted in Lake Athabasca in Saskatchewan.

The Basses

The trout may win the number-of-pages-written-about-them contest, but if the number of anglers counts for anything, then the basses (largemouth and smallmouth) are certainly the most popular game fish in America. The largemouth and smallmouth are not, however, true basses. That distinction belongs to the bass of Europe who had first dibs on the name. The American basses belong to the sunfish family. When you stop to consider this situation, though, the largemouth and smallmouth don't know or care what they are called; and the American basses, also known as the black basses, are pretty amazing game fish.

Figure 1-6

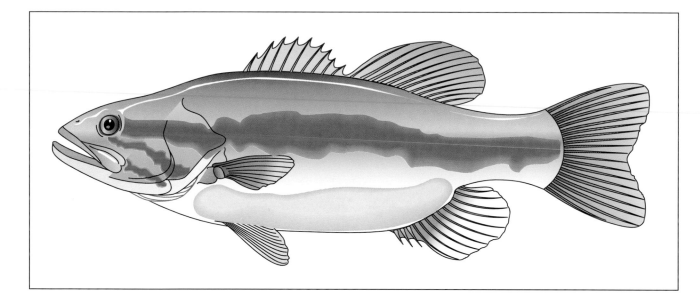

Largemouth

To my mind, no experience in angling is as thrilling as the moment that a largemouth bass takes a topwater plug. There you are, on a still summer day. Things couldn't be quieter. A few dragonflies buzz around a lily pad. A frog or two basks in the heat. You cast a topwater plug to the lily pad. You let it rest for a few seconds, and then you twitch it. You twitch it again. A fierce ripple knocks into your plug followed by the cause of the onrushing water, a ferocious largemouth that engulfs the plug. The instant it feels the hook, it begins to shake its head and jump or dive or both. An experience like this never ceases to thrill me, and it never ceases to take me by surprise.

The largemouth bass, originally a native of the Mississippi drainage and the southeastern U.S., was early recognized as a prime game fish and has since been transplanted all over. Lakes, rivers, streams, and brackish coastal water all have populations of largemouth.

They take lures, plugs, flies, plastic worms, real worms, crayfish, and crickets. In short, they are opportunistic feeders and are most catchable when the water is in the 65°F to 75°F range.

As shown in Figure 1-6, the jaw of the largemouth extends further back than the eye (which is not true of the smallmouth). The largemouth is usually dark gray to dark green in color with a dark band along the lateral line. The dorsal fin is divided into two distinct portions: hard spines in front and softer ones in the rear. The largemouth is also known as the bucketmouth because of his large mouth, which appears even larger when it attacks your lure, fly, or bait.

Figure 1-7

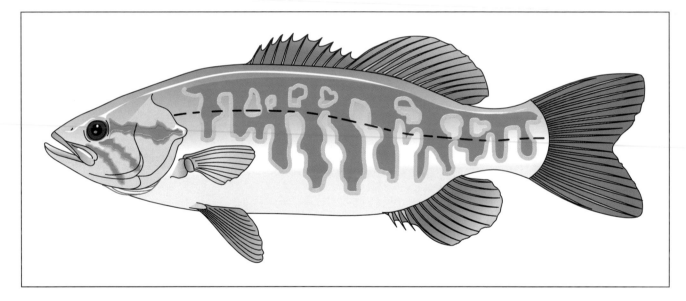

Smallmouth: The gamest fish

In what is perhaps the most-quoted phrase in angling literature, retired Civil War surgeon James Alexander Henshall called the smallmouth bass, "Inch for inch and pound for pound, the gamest fish that swims." This opinion set off a century of debates. Some said trout were the gamest fish; others awarded that honor to salmon. Bonefish, permit, snook, and tarpon all had their partisans, but no one ever said that Henshall was out to lunch for the high opinion in which he held the smallmouth, known affectionately as the *bronzeback*.

A true fish tale

It was rainy and windy on June 2, 1932, and nineteen-year-old George Perry was out before dawn with his fishing buddy Jack Page.

"My father died the year before," Perry later recalled. "I had my mother, two sisters, and two brothers. We lived three creeks further back than anybody else, and in those days it was a good deal of a problem just to make a living. I took money we should have eaten with and bought myself a cheap rod and reel and one plug."

Perry remembers that he wasn't feeling very lucky that morning on Montgomery Lake near Helena, Georgia. He tied on an imitation of the local bait fish, the creek-chub. A bass took the lure. Perry struck but couldn't budge it.

Then the fish moved, and Perry knew he was into a major bass. When it finally surrendered, even though it was enormous, Perry later said, "The first thing I thought of was what a nice chunk of meat to take home to the family."

Thankfully, Perry had the presence of mind to make a detour at the general store in Helena, Georgia, where the bass that he had pulled out of Montgomery Lake tipped the scales at 22 pounds and 3 ounces, duly notarized and witnessed. It is a world record that stands to this day.

With his place firmly enshrined in the history books, young Perry went home and prepared a very large largemouth meal for the family.

Like his largemouth cousin, the smallmouth is a native of the Mississippi drainage, which makes him a true heartland (or maybe "heartwater") fish. Where the largemouth likes slow or still water with lots of food-holding weeds, the smallmouth prefers clean, rocky bottoms and swifter water, ideally in the 65°F to 68°F range. Any warmer than 73°F and you can forget about finding a smallmouth. Lake dwelling smallmouth often school up, which means that if you catch one, you can catch a bunch. In rivers and streams, they are more solitary.Like the largemouth, the smallmouth is a pretty opportunistic feeder; but if you give smallmouth a choice, both crayfish and hellgrammites score well.

As shown in Figure 1-7, the smallmouth has a series of dark vertical bands along its flanks. The dorsal fin is one continuous fin (as opposed to the separate spiny and soft parts on a largemouth's fin). Another difference is that the smallmouth's upper jaw does *not* extend backward beyond the eye.

David L. Hayes caught the world record smallmouth in Dale Hollow Lake, Kentucky, on July 9, 1955. It weighed 11 pounds and 15 ounces.

TIP

How to pick up a bass

If you try to pick up a bass by grabbing its body, it is about as easy as trying to diaper an angry baby. The little suckers can *really* squirm. Even worse than babies, bass have spiny fins that can deliver nasty pricks. With a bass (and with many other soft-mouthed fish), however, you can nearly immobilize it if you grab it by the lower lip, holding it between thumb and fore-finger as shown in the adjacent figure. Be very careful of hooks, especially of lures that have multiple treble hooks. While picking up your catch by grasping the lower lip between thumb and forefinger works very well with bass, it has been reported that this technique doesn't work as well in singles bars.

Figure 1-8

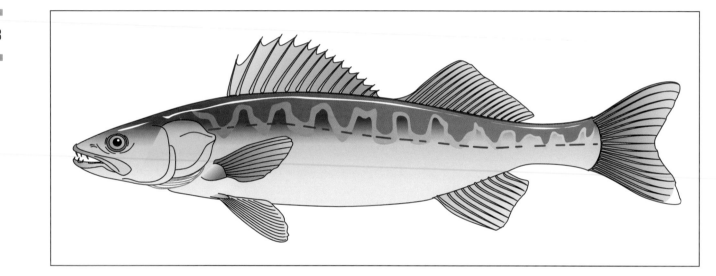

Good Eats: Walleye

On a number of trips to the state of Minnesota, more than one angler has said to me, "You can have your bass, and you can have your trout, but the walleye is the best eatin' fish there is, bar none!" Having tasted the flesh of this largest member of the perch family, I would have to agree that it ranks right up there with the best. Their excellent flavor may explain why walleye are often the preferred fish when they are available. In addition to being delicious, they are found in schools, hang out around underwater structures, and usually locate themselves near a drop-off. In other words, they behave just as a textbook game fish should behave — not a pushover, but not impossible to catch either. In many places, you can hear people talk about a walleyed pike, which is a local name for walleye but not an accurate one. The pike is a completely different animal.

The walleye requires a great deal of water and is rarely found in smaller lakes or ponds. Clear water and a rocky bottom are also high on its list of environmental preferences with water temperatures in the mid 60s (and never higher than the mid 70s) being optimum. It eats any bait fish that is available; and when they aren't, leeches are a terrific bait (as are worms).

Double dip

Question: How many people have both an element and a fish named after them?

Answer: One. His name was Deodat Dolomieu, and it happened in 1802. Dolomieu was a famous man-about-town in Paris as well as a mineralogist. The mineral dolomite was named after him. Dolomite is a favorite rock of anglers because its high limestone content makes for streams rich in food (which means *big fish*).

A naturalist named Lacepede also lived in Paris at that time. Someone had sent him a strange-looking 12-inch fish for classification. It was a smallmouth from Louisiana, which was still ruled by France in those days. This smallmouth had a gap in its dorsal fin, probably from a run-in with a pike or a beaver. Lacepede had never seen a smallmouth before, leading to his assumption that all smallmouth had teeny fins. So he called the new fish *Micropterus* which means "small fin" in Latin. Then he needed a second half for its Latin name, but nothing came to mind. Because Dolomieu was coming to dinner that night, Lacepede, at a loss for anything better to call the newly classified fish, decided to name it after his friend, which is why the smallmouth bass is known to scientists as *Micropterus dolomieu.*

The take of the walleye is subtle, not unlike the way a bass plays with a worm and then swims away with it before it finally decides to eat. The angler must give the walleye time to accomplish this maneuver before striking.

The walleye is a very light-sensitive fish, so although you may take one in shallow water, chances are that you will do this only in low-light conditions.

Mabry Harper holds the record for a 25-pound walleye caught on Tennessee's Old Hickory Lake on April Fool's Day, 1960.

As shown in Figure 1-8, the walleye is a torpedo-shaped fish with big eyes (hence walleye), a brownish-greenish color, and a white tip on the tail and dorsal fin.

Pike

For flat-out mean looks, nothing in freshwater rivals the looks of a pike, pickerel, or muskellunge. A long fish with big eyes, a pointed snout, and rows of stiletto teeth, the average pike looks like what you might get if you crossed a snake, a bird, and a shark.

Figure 1-9

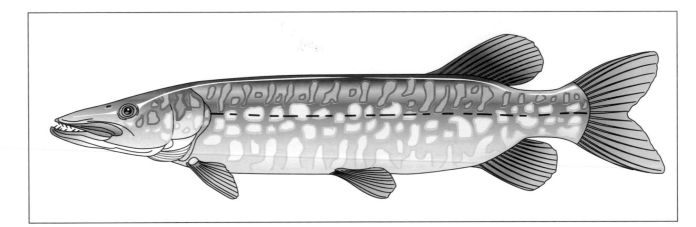

Northern pike

The most popular member of the pike family is usually known simply as the pike. It is also called a *northern* and is a native of the Great Lakes and its cooler tributaries.

Pike are clearly designed to attack and devour. One observer called them "Mere machines for the assimilation of other organisms." All forms of bait fish and game fish, birds, muskrats, frogs, snakes, snails, leeches, and anything else it finds within striking distance can (at one time or another) find its way into a pike's belly.

You are liable to find pike in weedy shallows where they wait for prey to ambush. As stealthy as a lion in wait or as swift as a springing panther, pike stalk and pursue their prey most actively at water temperatures in the mid 60s.

When fishing live bait, the angler must give the pike time. Sometimes it will snare a fish crosswise and take some time to maneuver it into swallowing position. Usually, a pike pauses right before it swallows any bait. When the pike pauses, strike.

When fishing with artificials, strike when the pike does. You will be rewarded by the sight of the writhing form of the pike rocketing from the water. Don't be fooled when the pike seems to surrender after a fierce, but short, initial run. As soon as it sees you or your boat, you usually get a very satisfying second (and even third) run. The Daredevle is an amazingly effective pike lure.

The world record belongs to Lothar Louis who took a 55-pound, 1-ounce pike on October 16, 1986 in the Lake of Grefeern, Germany.

As shown in Figure 1-9, the pike is a sleek and ferocious-looking predator.

Talk about sharp!

When landing a pike, be extremely careful of its sharp teeth. They are about the nastiest thing in freshwater fishing. (This advice goes for the pike's cousins, the muskie and pickerel.) As shown in Figure 1-10, the safest way to land a pike is to grab the fish by the eye sockets (the socket, *not* the eye!).

Figure 1-10

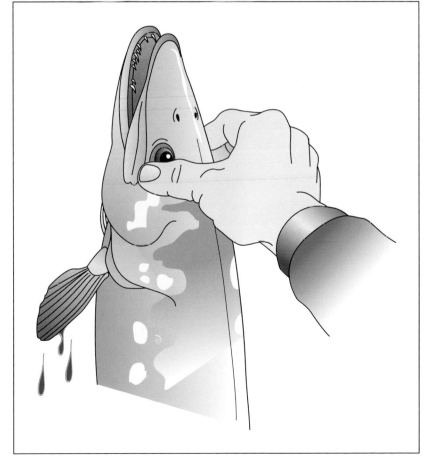

Figure 1-11

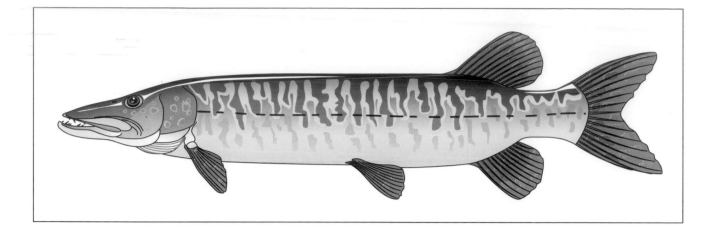

Muskellunge

If you are the kind of person who likes the odds in the state lottery, you should enjoy fishing for muskellunge. Your chances of winning the lottery and catching a muskie are roughly equal. (Actually, that is a bit of an exaggeration, but not by much.) The old-timers say that when fishing for muskellunge, it takes 10,000 casts for every strike. And then when you do get a muskie on, its teeth are so sharp, it can be so big, and its fight can be so dogged, that it takes brawn and skill to land one. If you manage to land a muskie, you have a real trophy.

Like the pike, the muskie (see Figure 1-11) hangs out in likely ambush spots: weed beds, deep holes, drop-offs, and over sunken islands. Although it spends most of its time in the depths, it appears to do most of its feeding in shallower water (at less than 15 feet). Optimum water temperature for muskies is in the low 60s.

The muskie is an opportunistic predator that strikes any number of baits or lures in any number of ways. Sometimes, a muskie strikes far from your boat, but sometimes it follows a lure right up to the gunwales. The muskie is completely unpredictable, and my advice to the beginning muskie fisherman is to get a guide or a local expert to take you until you get the hang of it.

The muskie is a northern fish, found in the upper parts of the Mississippi drainage, the St. Lawrence River, all over New England, and through most of Canada.

The world record, a 65-pound fish, was caught by Kenneth J. O'Brien at Blackstone Harbor, Ontario, on October 16, 1988.

A muskellunge's appearance is quite similar to that of a pike. You can't always be sure which is which unless you get pretty close to the fish, in which case you can see that the muskie, in contrast to the pike, has no scales on its lower cheek and gill covers. Its markings tend to look like dark bars or spots, but northern pike usually have lighter-colored spots that are shaped like beans.

Figure 1-12

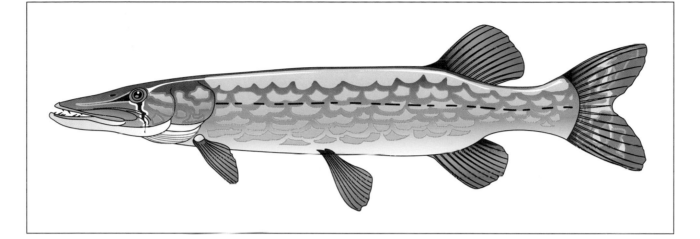

Pickerel

Though smaller than the pike and the muskie, the pickerel is (in every other way) as pugnacious and predatory as its larger cousins. When fishing a shallow bass pond on a day when nothing is happening, look for the arrowhead-shaped wake of a feeding pickerel. Whether the pickerel is cruising or sprinting from its lair in a weed bed, I think you will agree that it is exciting to watch a well-equipped predator going about its deadly work.

If you are working a spoon or spinner, you have a better chance if you retrieve your lure parallel to a weed bed, because you never know where a pickerel may be hanging out. Fishing for pickerel in water in the upper 60s is optimum.

The pickerel is to angling what the toy is to a box of Cracker Jack. The toy isn't the reason you buy Cracker Jacks, but it's a nice surprise when you get a good one, and many a bassless day has been saved by the voracious appetite of the pickerel.

The world record weighed 9 pounds and 6 ounces and was caught by Baxley McQuaig, Jr. on February 17, 1961 in Homerville, Georgia.

Figure 1-12 illustrates a chain pickerel, whose dark green side markings appear to line up like the links in a chain.

Figure 1-13

Pacific Salmon

Pacific salmon come upstream to spawn just as Atlantic salmon do. The Pacific salmon's flesh is pink, just like the flesh of an Atlantic. They even taste the same. But the six species of Pacific salmon are completely different animals than the Atlantic salmon, which is the only *true* salmon. The Pacifics are the much larger, mostly ocean-going cousins of the rainbow trout.

Some years ago, Pacific salmon were introduced into the Great Lakes to help control the spread of the alewife herring. The alewives were so plentiful and the salmon fed so well on them that the Great Lakes now hold the greatest fishery for both the coho and chinook sport-fisherman. This situation, though good for angling, shouldn't allow us to forget the alarming depopulation of these great game fish in their home range. Overfishing in their natural range has dangerously depleted them, as has the construction of dams.

In the Great Lakes, Pacific salmon are a big favorite among trollers. This method of taking fish, of course, requires a hefty boat and expensive gear, both of which are beyond the means (either financial or technical) of most beginning anglers, so I will just leave the fine points of trolling to the guides or your rich uncle.

Shallow-water and stream anglers have the most luck when the fish gather at stream mouths just before spawning. Fishing when the salmon are still *bright*, or fresh from the ocean or lake, can be great sport with these brawny, athletic fish. After they have been in the stream for any length of time, I find that landing even a 30-pound fish is about as much fun as lugging a duffel bag full of books up a steep staircase.

Pacific salmon like cold water, about 55°F. They move with currents and tides to maintain themselves in that *thermocline*, which is a big word meaning a region in a body of water with a specific temperature. A cold front may bring salmon close to shore. A wind may drive the cold water and the fish further offshore. When looking for them in a lake, using a thermometer to check water temperature is absolutely necessary.

As with many saltwater fish or as with fish that spend a good amount of time in saltwater (the term for fish that live in both fresh and saltwater is anadromous), the chinook and coho like flashy, bright-colored lures.

For bait, you may be hard pressed to find better than smelt or alewives. Salmon eggs are a fine choice as well. (Which always makes me wonder: Why would a fish want to eat its next generation?)

The world record chinook is 97 pounds and 4 ounces and was caught on May 17, 1985, on Alaska's Kenai River by Les Anderson. The record for the smaller coho is 33 pounds and 4 ounces; it was caught by Jerry Lifton on the Salmon River in Pulaski, New York, on Sept 27, 1989.

Figure 1-13 shows the coho and chinook salmon. The usually smaller coho has black spots only on the upper part of its tail, although the chinook's tail is spotted on both top and bottom. The chinook's dorsal fin is spotted; the coho's isn't. The gum in the lower jaw of the coho is grayish, but the same gum in the chinook is black.

Few fish are as delicious as the Pacific salmon (which is one of the reasons they are so heavily harvested by commercial fishermen). In many areas, particularly in the Great Lakes, fish can pick up toxic pollutants. The presence of pollutants doesn't make Pacific salmon less fun to catch, but eating fish from these waters is not a good idea. Always check the local health advisories before you take a fish for a meal.

Figure 1-14

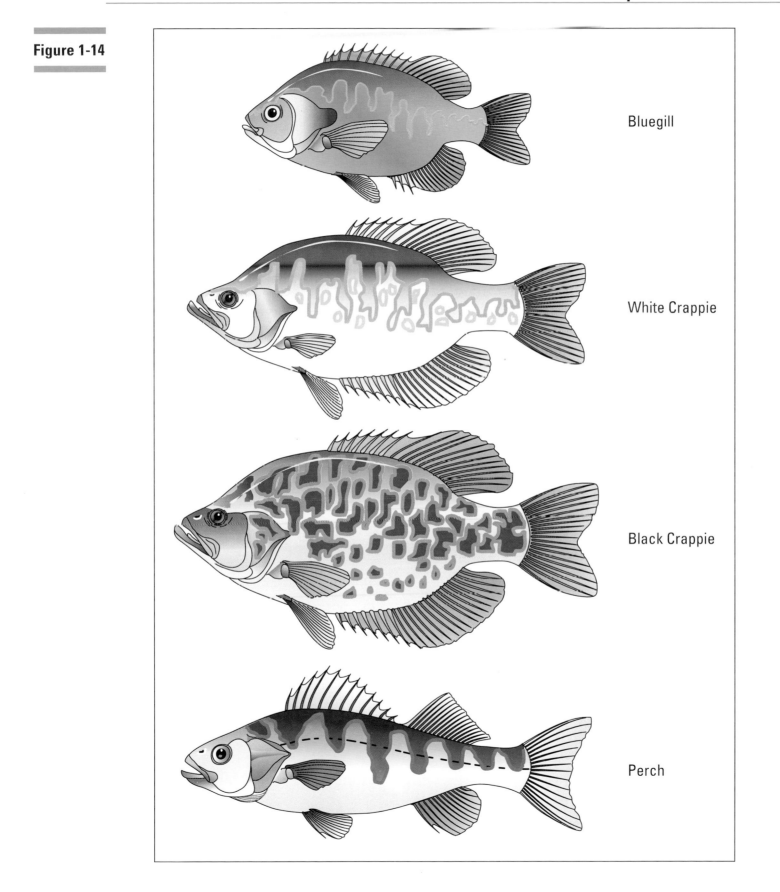

Bluegill

White Crappie

Black Crappie

Perch

Panfish

"Panfish" is really a catchall category that includes a whole range of fish, including most of the sunfish (except the largemouth and smallmouth bass) as well as crappie. Panfish are called panfish because they fit in a frying pan. This fact tells you something — namely, that panfish are good to eat.

In addition to edibility, another good thing about panfish is their "catchability." Whether caught with a cane pole, fly rod, or light spinning rig, panfish are extremely sporty. Worms, grubs, crickets, little spinners, popping bugs, dry flies, small jigs, bread balls, and corn are all effective panfish catchers. Since they are often the runts of the pond or stream, panfish will pretty much attack anything that looks remotely edible.

Figure 1-14 shows some of the more popular panfish.

- **Bluegill:** Sometimes known as the *bream*. It has a blue edge to the breast area and a dark ear flap and is probably the most-caught sport fish in America. The world record bluegill weighed 4 pounds and 12 ounces and was caught by T. S Hudson at Ketona Lake, Alabama, on April 9, 1950.

- **White crappie:** A very widespread fish all over North America. It is a terrific fish on a jig, but it, too, takes all kinds of bait and small lures. It thrives in silty and slow-moving water and has flourished in the impoundments that have been created in the south since World War II. The white crappie is the only sunfish with six spines on the dorsal fin. The world record white crappie weighed 5 pounds and 3 ounces and was taken at Enid Dam, Mississippi, on July 31, 1957 by Fred L. Bright.

- **Black crappie:** Prefers somewhat clearer water than the white crappie. Because of its mottled skin (the white crappie is more barred), a local name is also *calico bass*. The world record belongs to L. Carl Herring, Jr., for a 4-pound, 8-ounce fish caught at Kerr Lake, Virginia, on March 1, 1981.

- **Perch:** Both white and yellow perch are completely delicious fish. French chefs steam them in parchment and call the process *en papillote*. In Door County, Wisconsin, the old-time commercial fishermen would get the same effect bywrapping their perch in wet newspapers along with some onions, salt, and pepper and throwing them on the housing of their overworked diesel engines. Because these fishermen cooked on the domes of their engines, their meals were called "domers." The world record white perch was caught at Messalonskee Lake, Maine, on June 4, 1949 by Mrs. Earl Small. The world record yellow perch was caught in Bordentown, New Jersey, by Dr. C. C. Abbot in May of 1865. Now that's a long-standing record!

Figure 1-15

Catfish

Because most catfish feed at night, I suppose that their looks don't prove much of a drawback. Counting bullheads, there are more than 20 species of catfish in the U.S., and they are very popular because of their catchability, their accessibility, the relatively low cost of the tackle required to catch them, and lastly (but probably mostly) because of their wonderful taste. People usually eat crispy fried catfish the way they eat potato chips — until the last one is gone.

Because catfish are nocturnal feeders, they rely on touch, taste, and smell to identify food. So the general point that taste and smell of potential foods don't matter to fish — doesn't apply to the catfish. Some of the most nose-plug-requiring baits — called, appropriately, *stinkbaits* — attract catfish even though they smell as ripe as a marathoner's sweat socks.

When bait fishing, keep your bait on the bottom. That's where the catfish are. Lures are not that productive except with the channel cat, which is found in somwhat clearer moving water and often takes a deep-running plug, spoon, or jig.

Catfish are active in warm water and may be taken with water temperatures in the high 80s.

The world record blue catfish weighed in at 109 pounds and 4 ounces; it was caught by George A. Lijewski, March 14, 1991, on the Cooper River in South Carolina. The record channel cat, at 58 pounds, was caught in South Carolina's Santee-Cooper Reservoir on July 7, 1964, by W. B. Whaley.

Figure 1-15 clearly shows the difference between proper catfish and bullheads. Notice that both have long whiskers or *barbels*.

When you handle a catfish, it will "lock" together its pectoral and dorsal fins. The projecting spines are very sharp and carry a toxin. Though not fatal, a wound from these spines can be nasty and painful. If you are pricked while handling a catfish, treat the wound immediately with a disinfectant, as swift action often nullifies the poison. Apply a bandage. Your revenge on the catfish is that you get to eat him.

Figure 1-16

Shad

The shad, which is a large member of the herring family, lives most of its life at sea and returns to the river of its birth to spawn and die. This anadromous trait is not its only similarity to the more aristocratic salmon. The shad does not feed after it enters a river, but again, like the salmon, it can be induced to strike a brightly colored fly or lure. Nobody knows why they do this. I have read that they do it out of anger, or perhaps because they are reminded of food that they ate in the stream as a baby. Because most shad lures, which are called *darts*, look like really cheesy costume jewelry, you have to wonder about a shad's food memory.

I have fished for the smaller hickory shad in Florida in March. When hickory shad are in the rivers, thousands of white pelicans come in from the Atlantic to feast on their carcasses. In the northern part of the United States, the main river systems for shad anglers are the Delaware, Susquehanna, and Connecticut, where you can take them from a boat or while wading.

When playing a shad, remember that its mouth is very soft. Give it room to run. If you try to *horse* the fish (muscle it in), you will surely pull your lure or fly out. If you let it run, it will reward you with a number of beautiful leaps, just like a salmon.

The only type of shad for which world records are kept, the American shad, weighed 11 pounds, 4 ounces and was caught in the Connecticut River in South Hadley, Massachusetts, on May 19, 1986 by Bob Thibodo.

Both the American and the hickory shad have the large scales and deeply forked tails characteristic of the herring family, as shown in Figure 1-16. The hickory shad is generally smaller, and its lower lip extends out past the upper lip.

Figure 1-17

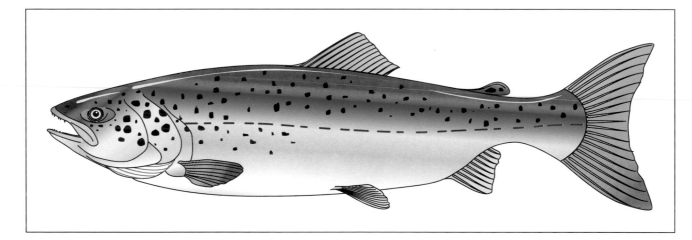

Atlantic Salmon

The Atlantic salmon is regarded by many as the aristocrat of fishes. Perhaps it has this reputation because you have to be an aristocrat to be able to afford a few days on one of the choice salmon rivers. Not surprisingly, with something that has become the sporting property of upper-class gentlemen, one is required to fish for Atlantic salmon with a fly rod; and on many rivers, one also has to rent a guide. Don't hold any of this against the salmon. He had very little to do with all the tradition surrounding him.

The salmon is a cousin to the brown trout but spends most of its time at sea (although a salmon's infancy is passed in a river, and it is to that river that it returns to spawn). The Atlantic salmon (shown in Figure 1-17) does not die after spawning once, so you may return a salmon to the stream after catching it and be confident that it may well return to create even more fish the following year. This practice is good because the Atlantic salmon is a very pressured animal. Perhaps if we conserve our salmon harvest now, they will return to the numbers they had back in George Washington's day, when they were so plentiful that farmers used them for fertilizer!

If plenty of action is what you crave, salmon fishing is not for you: Just one fish a day is a very good average on most streams.

Henrik Henriksen caught the 79-pound, 2-ounce world-record Atlantic salmon in 1928 on Norway's Tana River.

It Started with Adam (or shortly thereafter)

Although no one is sure exactly when people started to use fishing rods, we do know that Stone Age people used pieces of flint, bone, or wood to make fishing implements called *gorges*. Basically, a gorge was a double-pointed, bait-wrapped, narrow piece of flint, bone, or wood that was tied around its middle to its line. The fish would eat the bait, and (when the angler pulled on the line) the gorge would stick the fish's throat. It's probably safe to assume that those cave folk made these tools for fishing (otherwise it would have been a pretty big waste of time when they could have been out there chasing mammoths or giant sloths). The first real proof we have of people actually fishing with rods comes from drawings of the ancient Egyptians. Whether the "Phising" Pharoahs used bait or lures is an open question. We do know that the ancient Greeks fished. Homer, the author of The Iliad talks about people using an ox horn to catch "little fishes."

Those anglers of old used a wooden rod with a line attached to the end. It was very much like today's cane poles that many young anglers first use to fish for panfish at every lake and dock. We know that people were using reels by the 12th Century because pictures of rods and reels appeared in China shortly before Marco Polo visited there. And the art of flyfishing was already well advanced in England when, in the 15th Century, the most famous fisherwoman of all time, Dame Juliana Berners (an English nun), wrote her *Treatise on Fishing With An Angle*.

By the time that Izaak Walton wrote *The Compleat Angler* in the 17th Century, fishing knowledge about the fish that lived in the rivers of Europe was very advanced, but Walton never saw a rainbow trout, a largemouth bass, a bonefish, or a bluefish (all of which were first seen in the New World). Many of the fishing tools that are taken for granted today (such as more-advanced reels and rods made of newer materials) did not appear until the 19th and 20th Centuries. In the early 19th Century, the precision watchmakers of Kentucky perfected the modern bait-casting reel. A few decades later, in England, Holden Illingworth invented the spinning reel. The 20th Century has introduced such wonderful rod materials as fiberglass and graphite, which enable the modern caster to achieve distances that only a champion could have dreamed for in Walton's day. This century also saw the birth of the outboard motor, which works even better than the strongest rod in getting you within fishing range.

Chapter 2
Saltwater Fish

In This Chapter

▸ Staying uncut, unbitten, and in one piece around saltwater fish

▸ The best fish to cure the winter blues

▸ Why the striped bass is the trout of the ocean

Figure 2-1

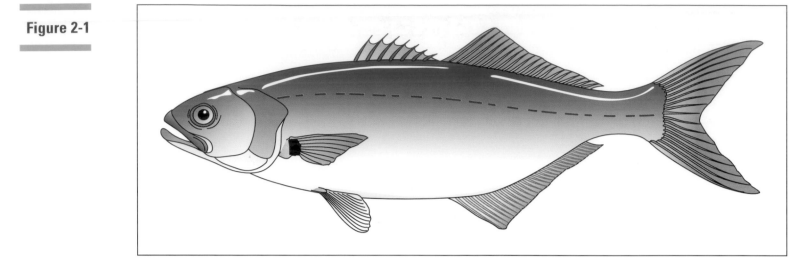

Bluefish — Good and Tough

The bluefish is Fishdom's version of that guy in the bar who asks every newcomer, "Hey, buddy, are you looking at me?" and then, without waiting for an answer, throws a punch. The guy can be big or little, can win or lose a fight, but he keeps coming back for more. Fighting is in his nature.

When blues are around, they hit anything — live bait or cut bait, plug, jig, or fly. Bluefish are excellent fish for newcomers because:

- They are very catchable — not real finicky about what you offer them.

- They are strong fighters, so even the novice can begin to learn how it feels to handle equipment in a tough fight.

- If you catch one, you will probably catch more because they usually travel in groups.

- They are delicious when eaten fresh. In fact, if you want a good lesson in the difference between fresh fish and funky fish, eat a fillet of bluefish on the day that you catch it and then leave one in the fridge for a few days. The fresh fish will taste light like a flounder. The refrigerated fish will have that oily taste that reminds me of last week's tuna salad.

Bluefish inhabit all of the world's oceans, spending a good half of the year in deep water. In the warmer months, when surf temperatures are between 55°F and 75°F, the blues follow bait fish into shallow coastal waters. When they do, they can be taken on all kinds of tackle with all sorts of bait, lures, and flies.

Bluefish have very sharp teeth, so whatever method of angling you use, you often find that you lose fewer fish if you use a wire leader. To avoid the chance of a bite, pick up a blue as you would a pike, by squeezing it behind the eye sockets. Use pliers to unhook a blue.

The world-record bluefish weighed 31 pounds and 12 ounces and was caught off Cape Hatteras, North Carolina, on January 30, 1972, by James M. Hussey.

Figure 2-1 shows a typical bluefish that, sure enough, looks kind of blueish on top when out of the water; but when you see them in the surf, they appear more coppery-green.

Figure 2-2

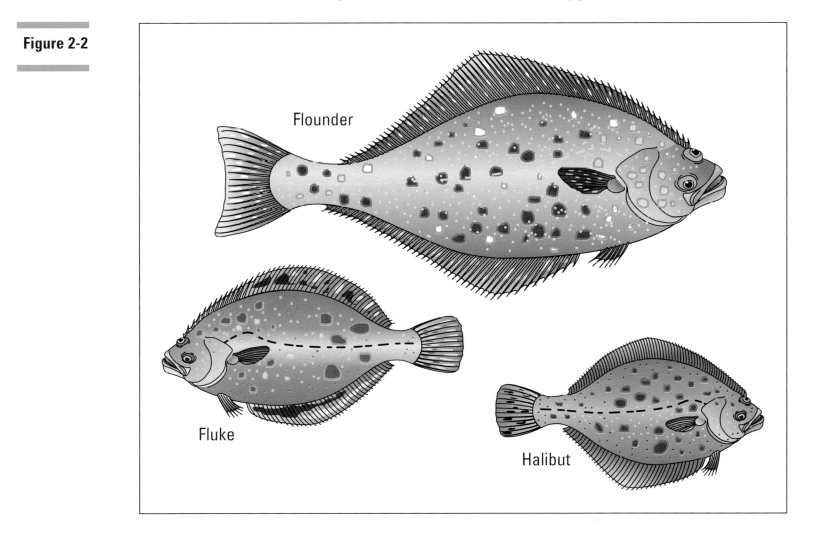

Flounder

Fluke

Halibut

Flounder, Fluke, and Halibut — Flat and Fun

In addition to being highly catchable and delicious, the flounder is one of the great early-season fish. When the first warm days of spring make it harder and harder to think about work, nothing is more pleasant than giving winter the kiss-off by catching a bucketful of flounder. A small boat and a simple fish-finding rig with a piece of clam on the hook are all you need to explore the protected bays and sandy coves where early-season flounder rest on sandy, muddy bottoms. They will strike your bait with a persistent tap-tap, your signal to rear back and strike. The type of rod you use isn't important. I have even caught flounder with a fly rod. Although tying a bait hook with a piece of bloodworm onto your expensive fly-rod outfit doesn't look very tweedy, it is fun.

The summer flounder is also known as the fluke. Its mouth and eyes are located on the left side of the fish. (The winter flounder is right-eyed and right-mouthed.) The fluke is a little more spunky than its cold-weather cousins; and although fluke, too, are found mainly on the bottom, they sometimes surprise you by chasing your bait when you are after blues or weakfish.

The halibut (shown with the fluke and flounder in Figure 2-2) is also a member of this family; and in contrast to the flounder, it will often use its broad, flat body to put up a terrific fight that may have you thinking that you are into a nice striped bass.

The world record fluke weighed 22 pounds and 7 ounces and was caught by Charles Nappi at Montauk, Long Island, on September 15, 1975. The record winter flounder, caught on Fire Island, Long Island, on May 8, 1986, by Einar F. Grell, weighed 7 pounds. The largest line-caught California halibut weighed 53 pounds and 4 ounces and was caught off Santa Rosa Island, California, on July 7, 1988, by Russell J. Harmon.

Figure 2-3

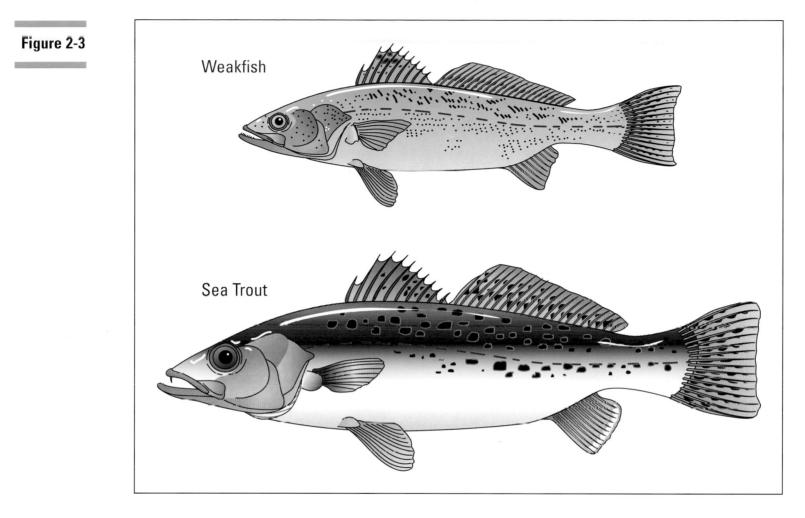

Weakfish and Sea Trout

These are two different but closely related fish. Neither of them is a trout, but their torpedo shape and spotted skin (as shown in Figure 2-3) are similar to a trout's. The weakfish is exclusively an Atlantic Seaboard fish, but the sea trout (or *speckled trout*) can be found from New England through the Gulf of Mexico. Weakfish and sea trout live side by side in the mid-Atlantic states.

Although no one has ever been able to explain why, weakfish, like many other game animals, experience sudden upticks and declines in population. Some scientists think that the weakfish/sea trout population fluctuation has to do with the availability of food in the deep-water wintering grounds somewhere off the Continental Shelf.

Bait fishermen do well with sandworms in the early season, switching to crabs and shrimp as the warm weather progresses. In the grass beds of Florida and the Gulf of Mexico, shrimp are far and away the preferred food; and the trick for the angler is to get a shrimp (or an imitation shrimp) to ride just above the top of the grass beds to avoid getting hung up if a fish strikes. Weakfish cruise these beds like white-tailed deer grazing in a pasture.

When fishing the bottom, a fishfinder rig with one or two hooks scores well for many anglers.

In the absence of any grass beds to hold shrimp, you need to fish tidal structures (rocks, inlets, drop-offs) just as you would with any other fish, looking for areas that are likely to carry bait fish in the moving tide. Surfcasters do well with spoons. Fly-rodding with shrimp imitations or poppers can be productive. No matter how you angle for weakfish, remember its name and how it got it: The mouth is soft; so even though it requires steady pressure to keep the fish out of the weeds, you also need a light touch so that you don't pull the hook out.

Two anglers are tied for the record weakfish at 19 pounds and 2 ounces. On October 11, 1984, Dennis Roger caught his in Jones Beach Inlet, Long Island, and five years later, on May 20, 1989, William Thomas caught his in Delaware Bay.

Figure 2-4

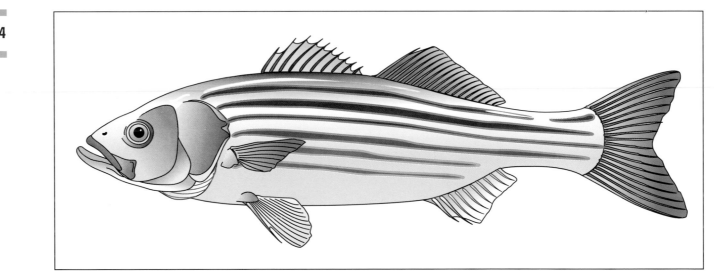

Striped Bass: A Silver Treasure

For the surf fisherman or fisherwoman, the striped bass (shown in Figure 2-4) is *the real thing*, the serious fish that makes your day. The striper, like the trout in freshwater, offers a special challenge and a special satisfaction. Like the trout, the striper can sometimes be caught without a great deal of thought on the part of the angler; but more often, stripers can be maddeningly selective. You can hear them slashing all around; but no matter what you throw them, they will not take because they are keyed in on one particular bait that is all-but-invisible to the angler.

Found from the Carolinas to Maine, and having been transplanted to the west coast and a number of reservoirs all over America, stripers are a favorite game fish. *Shoolie* (small) stripers can be caught on any form of light tackle. But the little guys aren't the only ones that run in schools. During the great migrations of spring and fall, stripers tend to travel in packs in which all the fish are of uniform size. (I have had days in early December off Montauk when they were all 30 inches long and gorging on herrings.)

Little fly, big fish

I became a believer in flies for stripers about ten years ago, around Thanksgiving time, when Jim Clark, a retired high school teacher in East Hampton, Long Island, called to tell me that the big ones were in right by his house near Georgica Beach. When I got there, the ocean looked anything but fly-fishable. The surf was high and roily and a strong in-your-face wind made casting very difficult.

"Ain't gonna happen, Jim," I said.

"Tie on a streamer and get out on that jetty quick, before the spinning guys beat you to it," he ordered.

Halfheartedly, more to please Jim than because of any faith in the fishing, I did as I was told and cast my small streamer into the heaving surf.

Pow! I was into a fish. After a beautiful fight, I beached a 36-inch bass. Jim, our buddy Peter, and I went on to catch nine fish in the next hour, all on two-inch-long Clouser's Minnows. Meanwhile, the conventional-tackle guys with the big surf sticks and the huge plugs were fishless, which speaks volumes about the importance of having the particular bait that the fish are taking (or at least something that looks like the right bait). In fairness to conventional-tackle anglers, I have noticed that many of them fish a bucktail dropper fly that looks just like a streamer; and often, on days when I do well on the fly, I have noticed that the dropper anglers do equally well.

Stripers take a variety of baits. Bait fish such as the bunker (also known as menhadden) produce well, as do herrings and bloodworms. Live eels can yield enormous fish. (While fishing with his dad in the autumn of 1995, Keith Meyer, the *New York Times* photographer who shoots the pictures for my fishing column, took a 64-pound striper on a live eel while fishing under the Triboro Bridge that connects Manhattan, Queens, and the Bronx.)

Plugs and spoons (the latter often fished with the hook buried in wiggly surgical tubes) both work well for stripers. You will do better fishing deep during the daylight. But surface lures are usually more effective in low-light conditions.

Fly-rodding for stripers is a fast-growing sport and one that has revolutionized fly-fishing in the northeastern U.S. Now, instead of making the long drive to crowded trout streams in the mountains, flyrodders are finding great sport close to home with stripers, often with major league fish in the 20- to 30-pound range.

Even though you may score on subsurface flies, nothing is more thrilling than watching a striper rush to engulf a popper. Even if surface fishing sometimes means catching fewer fish, the thrill is well worth the price.

My main advice for fishing stripers is this: When there is no visible surface activity, fish them with the same strategy that you would use for freshwater trout or bass. Like the trout, the striper hangs on the edge of the current and looks for feeding opportunities. For that reason, tidal rips are often the first place to look. And like the freshwater bass, the striper likes to hang around sheltering structures, picking off similarly-minded bait. In this case, jetties and rocky shorelines can produce good striper action. This affinity for a rocky habitat no doubt accounts in part for the name *rockfish*, by which the striper is known in the waters south of New Jersey.

The world record is held by Albert R. McReynolds, who caught a 78-pound, 8-ounce striped bass off Atlantic City, New Jersey, on May 7, 1992.

Figure 2-5

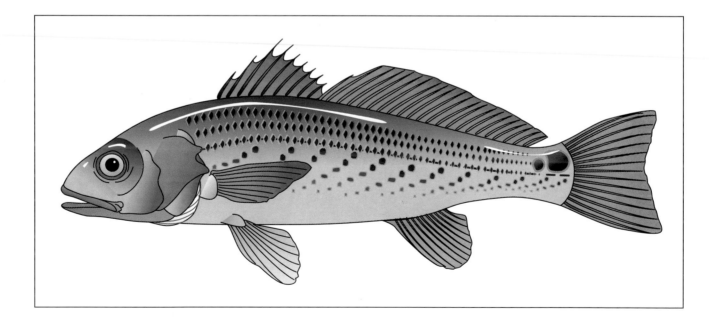

Redfish: A Cook's Tale

Thanks in part to the success of Louisiana Chef Paul Proudhomme's wildly popular recipe for blackened redfish, more people experience redfish on the plate rather than with rod and reel. In fact, Proudhomme's recipe caught on so well that the redfish were nearly fished out on the Gulf Coast.

TIP

Puffing for reds

With redfish and sea trout, I have found that if you don't see them on the grassy flats, that doesn't mean that they are not there. They could be following in the wake of a ray and picking up shell fish that the ray has stirred up as it cruises. Look for tight puffs of turbid water that indicate a recently-made cloud of mud. Cast into the trailing edge of the cloud and begin to retrieve line. I have caught many fish by this kind of blind casting. (Actually, it's not so much blind casting as it is blind hope!)

Also known as the *channel bass* or *red drum*, this crustacean-loving game fish is caught from New Jersey to Houston, Texas; but it is on the grass beds of Florida and the Gulf of Mexico that the redfish (shown in Figure 2-5) becomes a super-challenging opponent. And the shallower the water, the more thrilling the fight.

New Orleans redfish guide Bubby Rodriguez has taken me out to the shallow salt marshes where the Barataria Bayou eases into the Gulf of Mexico and has put me on 10-pound fish in less than a foot of water. This is hold-your-breath, one-cast fishing. It is also very demanding. You need to put the fly right in front of the fish's nose (within two inches). And you have to avoid spooking him with your line at the same time.

Actually, you don't so much *spook* as you *turn off* the fish. Often, a bad cast gets a look from the fish, after which it stays within casting distance but ignores you after you have been "made," to use a term that cops use for having blown your cover. The best fly for a red in Louisiana is a crab imitation. Shrimp also score consistently.

The world-record redfish weighed 94 pounds and 2 ounces and was caught off Avon, North Carolina, on November 7, 1984, by David G. Deuel.

Figure 2-6

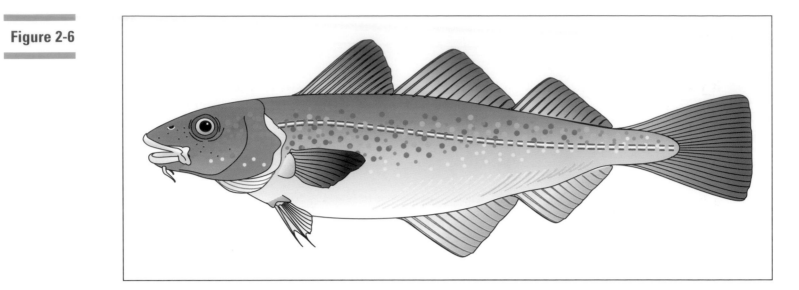

Cod

The cod, a delicious fish, is probably the most important commercial fish in history. Ever since Europeans arrived in the western hemisphere, commercial fishermen have made the long voyage from Europe to the fertile fishing ground of the St. Georges Banks. Their catch could be sold fresh or salted and dried. And cod, which prefer water temperatures in the mid 40s, can be taken through the winter when other fish desert the Continental Shelf for mid-ocean depths or southern waters.

Because you can catch cod in the cold months, they are a lifesaver for anglers on the Atlantic Seaboard. Party boat captains know where to find the wrecks that concentrate forage (bait) fish and the cod that feed upon them.

Cod angling is pretty much of the meat-and-potatoes variety: simple bait fishing or jigging just off the bottom. A sturdy boat rod with a bait-casting reel or a surf stick with heavy spinning tackle are the preferred instruments of most cod anglers. Because cod can often tip the scale at greater than 30 pounds, you want heavy line (at least 30-pound test).

The world-record Atlantic cod weighed 98 pounds and 12 ounces and was caught off the Isle of Shoals, New Hampshire, by Donald Vaughn on July 7, 1984.

Figure 2-6 shows an Atlantic cod with the telltale single *barbel* (whisker) hanging from its lower jaw.

Bottom Fish: Reef Fish

If you fish for blackfish (also called *tautogs*), groupers, snappers, or any one of the scores of delicious fish that fill buckets and bellies of anglers everywhere, you know that each species has its pleasures and subtleties. But they are all alike in that they are almost always fished with bait on or near the bottom, and the angling technique requires nothing more than positioning yourself over a fish, dropping your bait, and waiting for a bite. The trick is knowing where to fish and when. For this reason, my advice is this: Go out on a party boat (also known as a *head boat*) where, for a modest fee, you get tackle, bait, a ride to the fishing, and a boatload of experts who are more than ready to give you free advice. This is a great way to take the kids fishing with at least a reasonable expectation that they will catch fish.

Inshore Grand Slam: Especially with a Fly Rod

The tremendous upsurge in interest gave birth to the first generation of full-time fly-rod guides in many of these waters. Because their work takes them on the water so many more days than the average angler spends, and because their living depends on their clients catching fish, the successful guides have had to develop and refine new flies and techniques in a nation-wide flowering of angling creativity. The only parallel I can think of is the work done on trout fishing flies and techniques by the great Catskill guides and fly-tiers from the 1870s up through the 1970s (roughly from the time railroad brakeman Roy Steenrod tied the first Hendricksen dry fly, through the innovations of Lee Wulff, and up to the Comparadun series of Al Caucci and Bob Nastasi on the Delaware River).

These are good times in which to live and fish. In the same way that salmon and trout are at the top of the fly-rod angler's hit parade, the saltwater flyrodder also has a short list of great fish: bonefish, permit, snook, and tarpon. And by the way, I don't mean to exclude conventional-tackle fishermen. All of these fish can be taken on lures and baits as well.

Figure 2-7

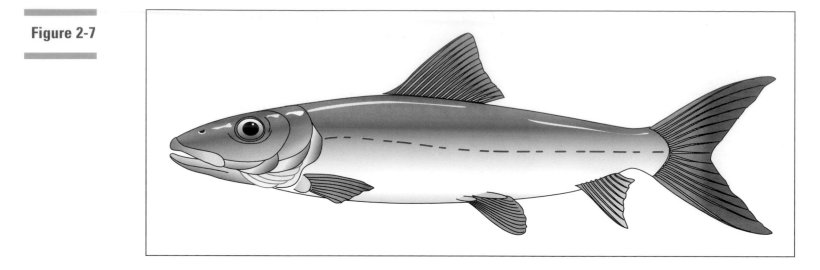

Bonefish: gray lightning

If one fish is responsible for kicking off the saltwater fly-fishing craze, it is this silver-gray denizen of sandy and coral flats in the world's warm-water oceans. From the west coast of Africa to the Caribbean to the paradise of the South Pacific, the bonefish is among the wariest shallow-water fish and, like the trout, responds well to the right fly, properly presented. A sloppy presentation, on the other hand, will cause the bone to turn tail and run for deep water with the speed of a cheetah.

The conventional angler can do well with live shrimp or an imitation-shrimp jig. The preferred fly-rod fly is a little shrimp imitation. The first trick to learn in fishing for bones is to see them. Initially, if you go with a guide (which is the *only* way for a new-comer to start bonefishing), you may feel that your guide is a liar or that you are close to blind because the guide may constantly call out, "Bonefish at 10 o'clock — 40 feet out."

You will see *nothing.* You will continue to see nothing for a long time, but trust me: Sooner or later, the bones will materialize. Eventually, you will be able to see the telltale black tip of their tails (and then their silver-yellow-green outlines) as they cruise. When you do, the trick is to cast four or five feet in front on the same line on which the fish is moving. In other words, lead the bonefish as a shotgunner would lead a duck or goose.

When the bonefish are feeding in shallow water, their tails will often stick up in the air. This activity is known as *tailing*, and it is to the bonefish angler what a rising trout is to the freshwater fisherman. I remember one Christmas, shortly after I was married, my wife and I went to check out Christmas Island, an atoll about 1,500 miles due south of Honolulu. The fishing was spectacular, and on Christmas Day, we were invited to the feast and singing contest at the main longhouse in the village called Banana (honest, that was its name). Because we were two of the only six non-Micronesians on the atoll, we were highly honored guests. The food was great; the singing was great. After lunch, as they smoked hand-rolled cigarettes of highly prized tobacco, the village elders began to tell tales of courage and adventure on the high seas. Just as they were getting to the classic legends, my guide showed up and said, "The tide is moving out, and there are five miles of tailing fish on the flat."

Right about there, I lost my interest in Tall Tales of the South Seas. We hightailed to the flat. As promised, the shallow water held ten thousand (or maybe ten million) bonefish, each with its tail waving in the pink-gold sun of the late afternoon. For the next three hours of the tide, we cast and caught, cast and caught. After you have been in and among tailing fish, catching one after another, you will understand the almost mystical awe that long-time bonefishers have for this fish in shallow water. One wrong move and you will spook hundreds of fish. But if you take your time and fish carefully, you can catch them until you decide to give up, which is one of the most rarely satisfying feelings in all of fishing.

With its big eye and downturned mouth, as shown in Figure 2-7, the bonefish is well designed to find food on the flats. I can't get it out of my mind, though, that despite its valor as a game fish, the eye and mouth give the bone a goofy look (as in Goofy, the cartoon character).

The world record bonefish was caught in deep water off the coast of South Africa on May 26, 1962, by Brian W. Batchelor. It weighed 19 pounds. Because he wasn't fishing for bonefish and it wasn't taken on the flats, I have always had a problem with this record, but my having a problem ain't gonna change things until you or I take a bigger one the "right" way.

Figure 2-8

Permit: wishful thinking

Only one fish may be harder to interest in a bait, lure, or fly than a permit — a dead fish. Although permit eat (otherwise how would they grow?), this broad-sided pompano is the most finicky fish when it comes to taking a fly. I have tried and tried and have never even *turned* one.

You should have more luck with bait or lures. Shrimp and crabs both produce well. In addition to being highly spookable, a feeding permit usually has its head down in the sand, looking for crabs. It concentrates on an area of just a few square feet. An angler's success in getting one to look up from feeding is like a parent's success when trying to get the attention of a teenager reading an Archie comic book: unlikely.

Permit are found in the same kinds of water and under the same condition as bonefish. Blistering as the bonefish may be in its initial run, the permit is its equal and then some. Add to this the fact that when a permit turns its body broadside to you, it can really put up some resistance. The result is a fish that many anglers classify as the hardest fight for its size.

I caught two permit on jigs at the mouth of the Boca Paila lagoons in Mexico. I was fishing with 12-pound test and a medium-action rod. The first fish took a good 25 minutes to land and had me running up and down the beach the whole time. I must have jogged three miles as the permit took me in and out of the surf. From the fight, I figured for sure that I had a 20-pound fish. But when the permit finally surrendered, it was a 5- or 6-pounder. I can only imagine what the feeling must be to catch a permit on a fly.

The world record permit weighed 53 pounds and 4 ounces and was caught in Lake Worth, Florida, on March 25, 1994, by Roy Brooker.

Often, the first thing you see on a permit, as shown in Figure 2-8, is the black tips of its fins as it cruises in shallow water. When permit flash by in large schools, their subtle gray-green coloration is very visible.

Figure 2-9

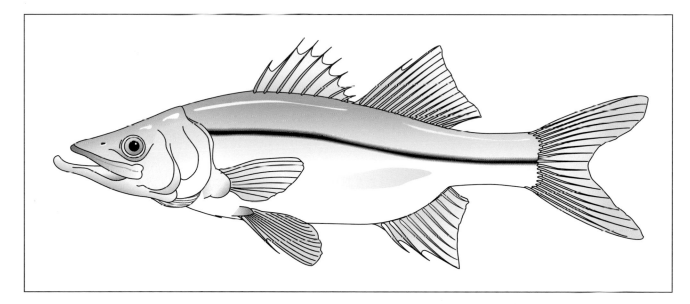

Snook: no schnook

A snook is a funny looking fish. Come to think of it, the word snook itself is pretty silly, too. A snook looks like a baby striped bass with shoulder pads. Perhaps this extra heft in the shoulders is what gives this resident of Florida and Central America such pugnacity when it fights, an experience that I can compare best to the struggle of a great largemouth bass. Although snook present a fair challenge to the angler, the commercial fisherman has little trouble in harvesting this delicious, white-fleshed fish, which is why it is relatively scarce in places where it was once abundant. I can recall fishing a river on the Atlantic side of Costa Rica and coming upon two Indians in a canoe piled high with snook — maybe 200 fish. These same Indians were out there every day, harvesting snook, so you can imagine how depleted the coastal creeks were becoming.

Killer gills

Dehooking a snook by holding it by the lower lip — just like you would dehook a bass — is best.

You should not put your fingers in gill covers which are super-sharp.

Thankfully, snook have been protected in recent years in the U.S. and have begun to make a comeback. They are like savage bass when they hit a plug, and I have also had great luck catching them with a fly rod and bass bugs. At night, when they congregrate under the lights of bayside docks, the fishing can be unbelievable. When the tide is running, the snook hang around the lights, picking off bait fish. By casting a streamer, first at the outside of the group and then further into it, you can take a half-dozen nice fish before you have exhausted the possibilities in any one *pod* (small group of fish).

Though snook make great eating, they are under so much pressure that I would advise you to keep them rarely, and only as a special treat. By returning them to the water alive, you can do your part to help bring back a classic sport fishery.

The snook shown in Figure 2-9 has the bright silver sides and clearly defined lateral line that are typical of this fish.

Figure 2-10

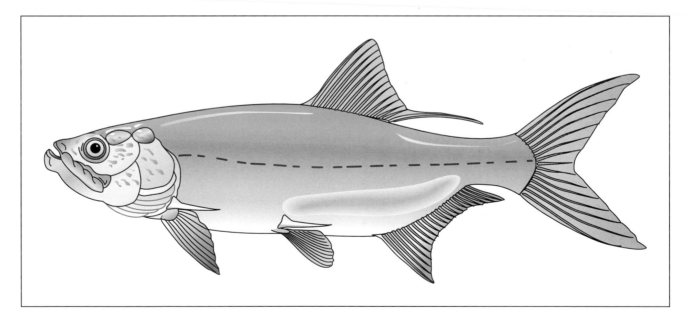

Tarpon: the silver king

The tarpon (see Figure 2-10) is a big fish — a very big fish — that can be taken on light tackle in shallow water. It can run forever and leap ten feet in the air, writhing as it does so. I can't imagine what more anyone could want out of an angling encounter.

Tarpon, which are very large herrings, have been taken on rod and reel for about a hundred years. Claims for having caught the first tarpon pop up in turn-of-the-century sporting literature with the frequency (and "checkup-ableness") of Elvis sightings. I am partial to the claim of Anthony Dimock, a tireless explorer of fishing opportunities in early Florida who reportedly subdued the first tarpon with sportfishing tackle in the 1880s. But then I am a fan of any guy who made and lost a couple of fortunes while maintaining his angling passion: Each time he was in the pink, he completely gave up Wall Street to become a full-time fisherman. His *Book of the Tarpon* has a remarkable series of photos of his fight with a huge fish, a fight that occurred nearly a hundred years ago.

Tarpon take squid, shrimp, or bait fish as well as plugs. I prefer them on flies, although I caught my first two tarpon (both better than 80 pounds each) with a Zebco spin-casting outfit, which goes to show that you don't need megabucks worth of tackle to enjoy catching this biggest of game fish encountered on the flats.

Whatever way you choose to fish for tarpon, heavy tackle is preferred because this fish requires all the force you can muster if you want to land one in less than half an hour. A long fight, in fact *any* fight, with a big tarpon can be very tiring; and the longer you have one on, the greater the chance you have of losing your fish to a shark. This has happened to me, and though exciting, it is also kind of a bummer. A strong rod quickens the fight in favor of the angler and also lets the angler strike hard and repeatedly in order to drive the hook home.

The great thing about a tarpon in shallow water is that it has nowhere to go but up, and this lack of room leads to a fight marked by thrilling acrobatic leaps. Many experienced anglers are happy just to hook and *jump* a tarpon and then to have it spit out the hook so that they can hook and jump another one.

With tarpon and other really big game fish, there is no question in my mind that you should hire a guide until you are a real veteran. In addition to everything else (like knowing where the fish are and having the right heavy-duty gear), the experienced guide knows how to tie a super-heavy shock leader with the Bimini Twist knot, a complicated knot that, as far as I can tell, requires the knotter to be able to execute a series of ten consecutive somersaults and a double axle from a sitting position.

Figure 2-11

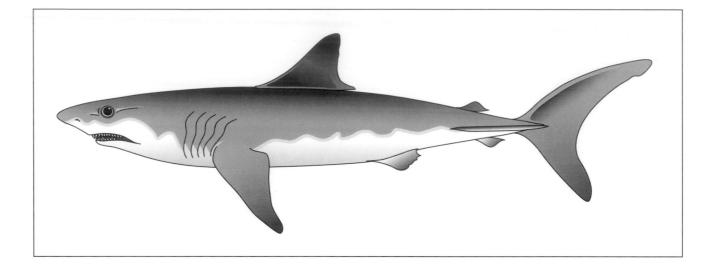

Sharks: Underwater Hell's Angels

Because sharks (shown in Figure 2-11) have such a well-deserved reputation as ruthlessly efficient predators, they appeal to many anglers' macho instincts (fisherwomen can have macho instincts as well as men). To be locked in combat with a deadly killing machine is sure to get your juices running; in fact, such combat is probably the reason why we evolved juices in the first place. Add to this the big buildup that shark fishing got as a result of the movie *Jaws*, and you have the explanation for the boom in shark fishing of the last 20 years.

In that time, charter captains have become more savvy, and equipment has evolved so that more anglers are taking more sharks than ever before. The consequence is that there are fewer sharks to be had. My strong recommendation is that you keep no more than one shark a year and return the rest after tagging.

Your captain will set you up with tackle — usually pretty hefty stuff. The captain will also have a good idea about how to play wind, tide, and underwater structures to give you the best shot at a shark. Still, *you* have to do the catching.

The most critical maneuver is the strike. *Don't* strike the instant that your bait is taken. Give the shark time to swim with it, play with it, and take it deep. Reel down as you would with a freshwater bass (in other words, lower the rod as you reel in). Point your rod tip at the fish; and when you *come tight* (that is, you have recovered all the slack), rear back and really slam that hook home. Then hold on. The shark will give you a tenacious and long fight. If you are lucky enough to hook a mako, you will be rewarded with a series of dazzling leaps — often 10 or 15 feet in the air! The fight can last a half hour or three hours. Either way, you will be tested to the limits of your endurance. And when you want to give up and cry uncle, remember that you are the one who wanted to go fishing in the first place; so, when you finally have a fish, don't weenie out.

Sharks come in many species and sizes. You can catch a 1-pound blackmouth or a 1-ton great white. Anything in the 100-pound class is a bona fide big game animal.

They're only dead after you cook them

After you catch a shark and bring it on board, you may want to get an up-close look of your prize catch (or even a photo of yourself holding the fish). Don't do it! Plenty of supposedly dead sharks have taken a nasty chunk out of anglers trying to handle them. And even if the teeth don't get you, a hook may, or a thrashing tail could give you a good knock. Leave the shark handling to the pros.

Figure 2-12

Tuna

If striped bass are like white-tailed deer — a fair-sized quarry, with the occasional trophy-sized one thrown in — then tuna are like elk. Tuna are big — truly one of the world's great big game animals. Because you can catch them within a few hours of New York City, people tend to discount what rare prized game they are. But to someone in Nairobi or Berlin, a giant tuna is as much an exotic trophy as a water buffalo or a red stag is to a New Yorker. Furthermore, like the elk and other large herd animals, the tuna undertakes a semi-annual migration: In autumn, it travels from its summer grounds off the northeastern coast of North America to its winter quarters in the depths of tropical seas. In the spring, it returns northward.

The ultimate in tuna fishing is getting out to deep, blue water, 70 to 100 miles from shore, where whales and dolphins and sharks are also found. You may just as well be 1,000 miles from shore. It feels like a whole other world out there.

Like sharks, tuna (shown in Figure 2-12) come in all sizes. All of them fight beautifully. When it comes to pure fight, my favorite fly-rod fish is the false albacore at about 8 or 9 pounds. The much larger yellowfin and bluefin are definitely heavy-tackle, charter-boat-type fish. These fish range from 30 pounds up to 1,000 pounds plus.

Giant tuna have been taken on rod and reel for only a little more than half a century. The legendary Lee Wulff told me that he once entered a rod-and-reel tournament held by the government of Labrador in the late 1930s. When he won the contest with two giant bluefins, the provincial governor noticed Lee's picture in the *New York Times* and offered him a plane and financial backing to explore angling opportunities in Labrador. Wulff learned to fly, got his pilot's licence, and in the following few years went on one of the great fishing exploration trips of this or any century, opening many new lakes and rivers for anglers seeking giant brook trout, huge pike, and Atlantic salmon.

Overfishing and the huge upsurge in popularity of sushi (a Japanese delicacy made from raw tuna) have made tuna so scarce that a big fish can fetch $10,000 to $20,000 at the dock. Here, as with all big game, only strict regulations and a catch-and-release conservation ethic can preserve the thrill of tying into one of the giants of the ocean.

The world record bluefin tuna was caught at Aulds Cove, Nova Scotia, by Ken Fraser on October 26, 1979. It weighed 1,496 pounds. The record yellowfin, at 388 pounds and 12 ounces, was caught at Isla San Benedicto, Mexico, on April 1, 1977, by Curt Wiesenhutter.

Figure 2-13

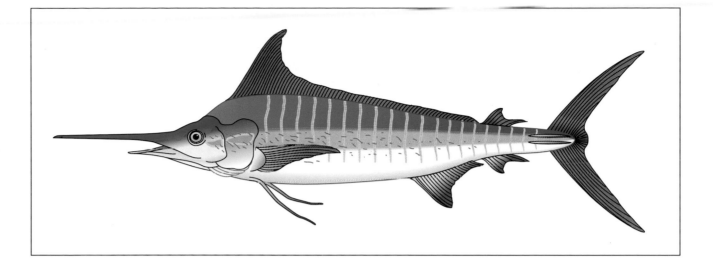

Marlin

The marlin is *it* — The Big One. It leaps like a tarpon, runs line like a bonefish, and dives like the stubbornest brown trout. The only difference is that a small black or blue marlin is the size of a defensive tackle on the Dallas Cowboys, and a big one is the size of a pickup truck. If you want to take your measure against a fish, the marlin can test all of your angling skills (and your strength and endurance, too).

The white marlin, the smallest of the group, is an Atlantic fish. The blue marlin is both an Atlantic and Pacific fish, and the black is a Pacific fish. Bait fishing is the most effective angling method. Bonito and wahoo are the baits I have used the most. Trolled lures can be very effective, and marlin have even been caught on flies. This last method involves a very intricate angling method. The fish is *teased up* (induced to strike) with a hookless lure that makes a great deal of commotion. When the marlin is within casting distance, the teaser is cranked in, and the fly is presented to the fish. This same teasing technique is also used with conventional tackle.

If and when you do catch a marlin, bear in mind that they must have evolved that big sword (shown in Figure 2-13) for something. It packs a wallop, so my advice is this: Don't touch it if the marlin is alive and assume that the marlin is alive until somebody tells you otherwise.

The world-record black was 1,560 pounds and was caught off Cabo Blanco, Peru, on August 4, 1953, by Alfred C. Glassell, Jr. The record blue was a leap year fish at 1,402 pounds and 2 ounces, caught by Robert A. Amorim on February 29, 1992, in Victoria, Brazil. The record white was 181 pounds and 14 ounces and was caught on December 8, 1979, by Evandro Luiz Coser, also in Vitorio, Brazil.

Chapter 3
· · · · · · · · · · ·
Just a Few Knots

The 5th Wave   By Rich Tennant

The fishing lures of Capt. Ahab

In This Chapter
· ·

▸ The three most important knots
▸ A couple of other pretty important knots

· ·

So Many Knots, So Little Time

At last count, the experts in knotology say there are about 3,000 different knots. I do 90 percent of my fishing with three knots. These three knots are not the prettiest knots, but they are the easiest, and they are as strong as any knot you can name.

In this chapter, I have tried to describe some knots (including my three favorites) and illustrate them. (Actually, I didn't really illustrate them myself. I can't even draw a smile button. The figures in this chapter, like all the other figures in this book, are the creations of Ron Hildebrand, who gets a big vote of thanks from me!) But great illustrations and the clearest descriptions are, at best, just a guide. Whenever I read angling books and attempt to learn the knots shown in them, I find myself trying to look upside down or doing almost-impossible contortions. The long and the short of knot-tying is that you just gotta do it (and do it again and again and again).

I will say this: Every knot has a logic to it, and every time you learn a new knot, there comes a point in the learning process when you will understand *why* the knot works and *what* it does.

Some knot-tying words

Most knot-tying instructions use a few standard terms. These terms are pretty self-descriptive, but just to make sure that we are all on the same page, here they are:

Tag end: The end of your line. This is the part that does the knot-tying. When you are finished tying, the tag end is the sticking-out part that you clip.

Standing end: The rest of your line. You tie the tag end around this.

Turn: Sometimes called a wrap. A turn is created when you pass the tag end through one complete turn around the standing end.

Figure 3-1

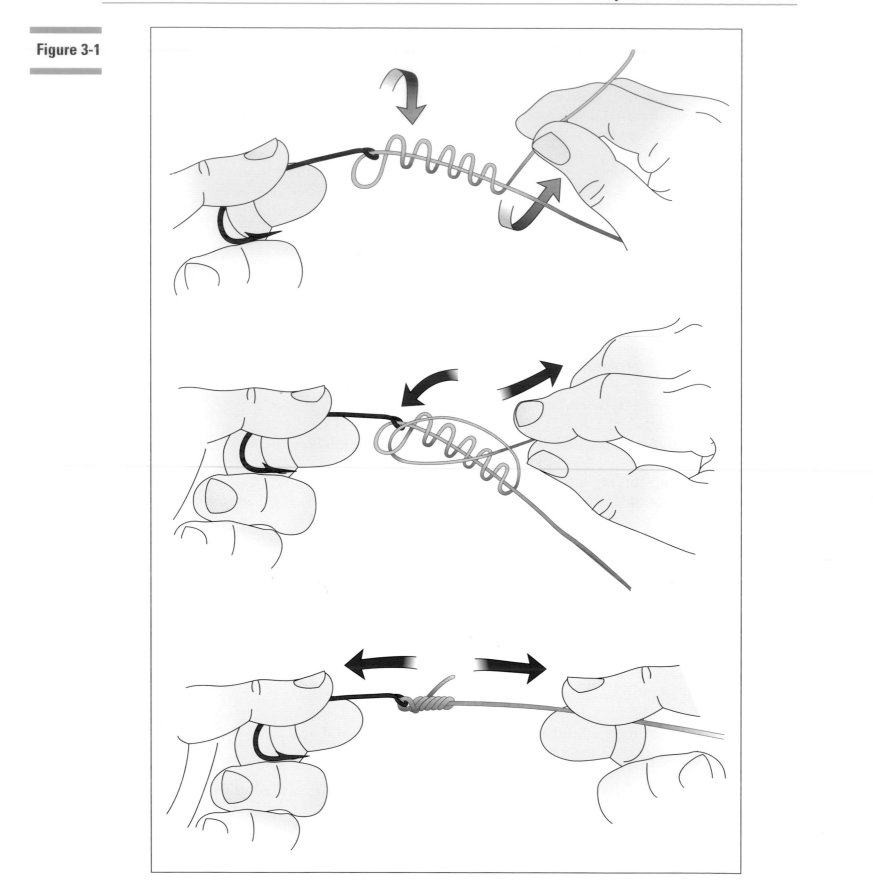

The Fisherman's knot

The real name of this knot is the *Improved Clinch knot*. But back when I started fishing, many people called it the Fisherman's knot because every angler knew how to tie this knot, and it was often the first knot they learned. Use the Improved Clinch knot to attach your line to your hook.

If a knot ever fails on you, 99 times out of 100, the place where it fails is right next to the hook, so the knot you use at this critical place should be the most reliable one that you can tie. Since I began fishing, I have read many claims for many other knots; some of the claims were quite learned and passionate. But guess what? The Fisherman's knot still gets the nod from me. Here's why:

A few summers back, my oldest daughter, Lucy, went to The Catskill Fly-fishing Center. This organization's wonderful two-day introduction is held on the Willowemoc River, which is about as close as you can get to holy water in fly-fishing. You may think that the folks at the center taught Lucy some knot that could only be learned by people who had a reading knowledge of Latin. Wrong. They taught her the Improved Clinch knot, and they called it the Fisherman's knot.

To tie the Improved Clinch knot, as shown in Figure 3-1, follow these steps:

1. **Run the tag end of the line through the eye of the hook and pull 8–10 inches of line through the hook eye.**

2. **Wrap the tag end around the standing end for five wraps or turns.**

3. **Now pass the tag end through the loop next to the hook eye.**

   You will have formed another loop that includes your wraps.

4. **Pass the tag end through that loop.**

5. **Wet the loops with some saliva to lubricate the knot.**

6. **Hold the tag end and standing end in one hand and the bend of the hook in the other; then *pull with steady pressure*.**

   If you are not sure about safely holding the hook, grip it firmly but not super firmly with needle-nose pliers.

7. **Tighten slowly.**

  ▮ ▸ **8. Clip the tag end so that only 1/8 inch is left.**

A standard fingernail clipper is a great tool for making a clean final cut on the tag end. Here's another tip: Leave the remaining tag end about 1/4-inch to 3/8-inch long; then touch the very tip of the tag end to the hot end of a lit cigarette (or a just-blown-out match) in order to create a ball on the end of the line, which prevents the tag end from pulling out under stress.

Figure 3-2

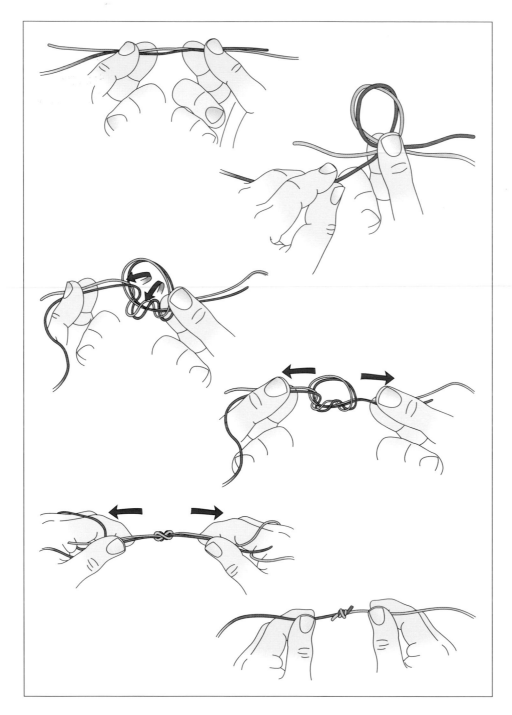

TIP

The Surgeon's knot

Twenty-five years ago, I was on the Beaverkill River in the Catskills. No one was catching fish except for this one silver-haired guy. He laid out line like he was shooting a laser. He caught fish after fish. After a while, he left the stream. When he passed me on the bridge, I complimented him on his fishing prowess, and I offered him a pull of bourbon that I had in a flask to ward off the early spring chill. As we talked, I learned that he was the well-known fly-fishing author, Doug Swisher.

While looking at his fly, I noticed the ugly knot joining the last length of tippet to his leader. I asked about the knot, and, by way of reply, Doug demonstrated the Surgeon's knot. This knot got its name because it's the same one that surgeons use to close up their handiwork. I use it to join two pieces of line that are close to each other in diameter. The Surgeon's knot takes the place of the more-complicated Blood knot (which is not described in this book), but it is not as pretty.

TIP

You have *two* hands and *ten* fingers

When tying knots, remember that there is no law against changing hands while you are tying. Sometimes you can hold the standing end in one hand, and sometimes you can hold it in the other. If you try to tie a knot by starting with the standing end in one hand and keeping it there until the end, you will end up in a pretzel position. Again, try to understand how the knot functions; then use whichever hand works best at the moment.

More than one fly-fishing buddy has turned his nose up at my scraggly looking Surgeon's knot. Hey, it may not *look* great, but it *works* great. And if a surgeon feels that this knot is dependable enough to close up a wound, I am willing to trust it to haul in a catfish.

To tie the Surgeon's knot, just follow these steps:

1. **Lay about 10 inches of tag end on top of your standing line, as shown in Figure 3-2.**

2. **In one hand, hold about four inches of standing line and the tag end and make a loop.**

✓ **3. Pinch the loop together between thumb and forefinger.**

✓ **4. Take the other end of the tag end and the end of the standing line and, passing it through the open loop, wrap them twice around the two strands of your loop.**

✓ **5. Using both hands, pull evenly on all four strands.**

✓ **6. Wet the knot with saliva when you are just about ready to finish pulling the knot tight.**

✓ **7. Clip the tag ends.**

After a little practice, you will see that the Surgeon's knot is easy to tie. After you know how to tie this very well, practice tying it in a dark room or step into a closet and tie it. Knowing how to tie a simple knot in the dark can be a handy skill. (I leave it up to you to explain things when someone opens the closet door and finds you standing there with two lengths of fishing line in your hands.)

A perfect match

If you use the Surgeon's knot to create a tapered fly leader, you want to make sure that you have an *even* taper. If one piece of line is much thicker than the piece to which it is joined, you will wind up making a sloppy, fish-scaring cast.

Here's the easy way to see if one piece of leader overpowers the other in any connection you make. When you have two pieces of mono that are matched (close, but not quite the same, in diameter), they make a nice even curve (a smooth oxbow loop) when you push them together. When the thicknesses are unmatched, the weaker of the two lengths of leader collapses or pushes in against the stronger length. If your fly leader isn't turning over (unrolling completely) then you are probably connecting lengths of line that are unmatched.

Figure 3-3

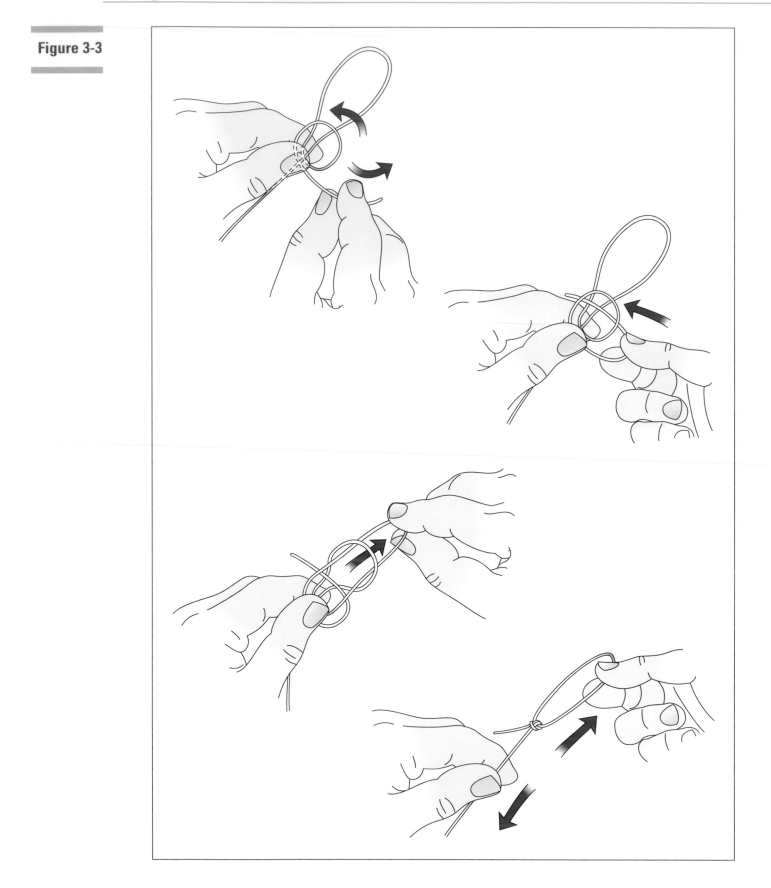

The Perfection Loop

The Perfection Loop is another of those less-than-gorgeous-looking knots. I use it to connect my leader to the butt of the fly line. I also use this loop to make droppers for 8-ounce sinkers when I am fishing live eels for stripers 80 feet down in the currents of Hell Gate on the East River in New York. In other words, the Perfection Loop is a versatile knot. It is very fast to tie, and (like the Surgeon's knot) you can do it all by feel in almost total darkness.

Check out Figure 3-3 and follow these steps to tie a Perfection Loop:

 1. **Create a 11/2-inch loop and pinch between thumb and forefinger.**

 2. **Repeat the action, creating another smaller loop around the first loop and pinch again.**

 3. **Run the tag end between the two loops and continue to hold everything pinched together.**

 4. **Pull the second loop through the first loop and start to tighten the knot, providing the final tightening with a pair of pliers.**

Chapter 4

Bait Casting

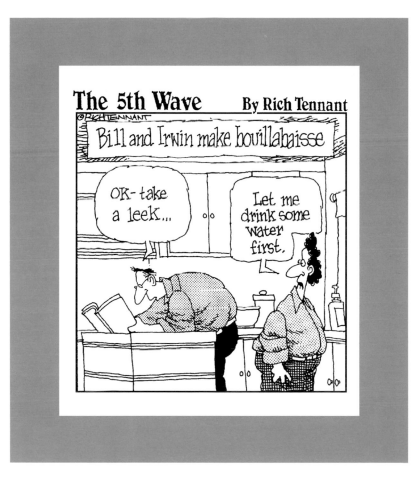

In This Chapter

▸ Casting without backlashing (most of the time)
▸ Underhanding, sidearming, and other contortions
▸ Why I love my thumb

Think of a fishing rod as a new part of your body. To become proficient at any new skill, you have to educate your body. Of course, when you learn to walk and everyone laughs at you because your walking style looks really cute, that's kind of fun (if you are one year old). When you are older and are learning how to cast, you don't want to be laughed at and told that you're cute. You want to catch fish.

The Purpose of the Cast

If you could walk up to a fish and drop a lure and line in front of its mouth, you wouldn't need to cast. But you can't do that because fish are not that suicidal. They head for cover long before you can get within arm's length of them. The *cast* is the long-distance method you use in order to deliver the fly, lure, or bait to a spot where a fish may be enticed, rather than alarmed, by your offering. So in addition to *delivery* (which is concerned with *where* your hook lands), casting also involves *presentation* (which is *how* the bait, lure, or fly lands).

Only Three Factors

Casting involves three elements: the rod, the reel, and the line.

The rod

All casting — bait, spin, and fly — requires the ability to handle a rod and to get it to flex and release your offering in a controlled way.

The reel

In addition to proper handling of a rod, bait casting (and spinning) require proper handling of the reel and the line as it comes off the reel.

Bait casting is difficult to master initially. Everybody has a natural tendency to produce depressing backlashes, but proper casting technique isn't rocket science. With a little persistence and a healthy dose of caution, you can actually be up and running pretty quickly. After that, it's a matter of finesse, and that comes with practice.

The line

Line handling, while critical to the flyrodder, is less so to the baitcaster. Once the lure or bait is cast, there isn't a whole lot of line handling involved.

Casting and Hitting a Baseball

There is a fourth element in the casting equation — *you*. The closer you get to making your cast into one seamless motion — from body to rod to line to lure — the more effective you can be. The one big concept I can give you is this: Think of what's going on at the end of the line. This notion is something I learned while writing a magazine story about Charley Lau, the great batting coach who has had such an influence on modern hitting technique. Lau used to tell his hitters to "think the ball straight up the middle, over second base." His theory was that if a batter did that, he would be more likely to make proper contact with the ball. And by making proper contact, he would get more hits (and even the occasional home run).

Charley was also a great fisherman. In fact, in the years between retiring as a major league catcher and starting as a batting coach, he spent some time as a fishing guide in the Florida Keys. He applied the same spirit of analysis to casting. Every angler tends to think about what is happening right next to his or her hands, he said, where the rod and reel are. But the critical point is farther away — way out there at the end of the line. If you think about where your bait, lure, or fly is and *what it is doing* in the water, you can affect your cast in a positive way.

If you don't think the body mechanics of baseball and fishing are related, you should look at a video of the casting technique of baseball great Ted Williams. The way that The Splendid Splinter handles a fly rod and line is the same as the way that he handled a bat — smoothly, fluidly, powerfully, and accurately.

Bait Casting: It's All (Well, Almost All) Thumbs

Each type of casting has its own techniques. Bait casting is often very frustrating at first, but, as they say, "No pain, no gain."

Figure 4-1

The overhand cast

This is the cast that you will use in most situations. Before you move on to the more specialized casts, really try to get this one down pat.

  ✔ **1. As seen in Figure 4-1, the overhead cast begins as you grasp the rod with the crank facing *up*. The shoulder of your casting arm is pointed toward the target.**

  ✔ **2. Put the reel into *free spool* by disengaging the *clicker*.**

  You should have anywhere from two to six inches of line hanging out of your *tip top* (the top line guide on the rod). Keep your thumb on the spool so that it doesn't move.

  ✔ **3. Point the rod at your target.**

  Your body is aligned so that, if you are a right-handed caster, your left foot is forward. (If you are left-handed, your right foot is forward.)

  ✔ **4. *Before* you start the lifting or *backstroke* of your cast, position the rod at about a 35-degree to 45-degree angle.**

  This action will put some flex into the rod as you begin your cast. Keep your thumb on the reel and keep the reel locked all through the backstroke.

  ✔ **5. Crisply lift the rod, applying power until the rod is pointed at the 12:00 position.**

  The momentum of the cast will bend the rod farther backward, putting flex into the rod. The rod is designed to do this. You don't need to apply any more power on the backstroke. If you do, you will *overload* (develop too much torque on) the rod.

  ✔ **6. As soon as you stop the backstroke, begin the forward *power stroke*, releasing thumb pressure as you do (so that the lure can pull line off the reel as it travels to the target).**

  The power stroke ends when the rod returns to the original 35-degree to 45-degree position.

  ✔ **7. Continue to allow the line to unspool.**

This is the key part of the cast and the part that is most prone to backlashing unless you successfully complete Step 8.

▶ **8. As the lure nears the target, apply more and more thumb pressure so that the reel gradually slows down and comes to a complete stop just as the lure hits the water.**

If you don't do this, the reel will keep spinning as the lure hits the water, a sure recipe for a backlash.

The way to learn bait casting with minimum heartbreak is to try it a little bit at a time:

▶ **1. Before you make your first cast, get yourself up to Step 4.**

▶ **2. Next, while holding the thumb on the spool, lift the rod another 15 degrees or so.**

▶ **3. Release some thumb pressure so that the lure descends pretty freely; then, as it does, put more pressure on the spool to slow it down so that it stops completely by the time the lure hits the ground.**

After you have accomplished this smoothly, you will have at least an idea of the thumb control technique needed for real casts. Try short casts at first, using the thumb as a brake (better to use too much braking rather than too little when you start out). Your casts may be short of the mark this way, but you will not have a backlash. As with all the casts discussed in this chapter, I recommend that you practice on a lawn before you try it out under combat conditions. The more you continue practicing your technique on a lawn in between fishing sessions, the better you will become.

The sidearm cast

When Joyce Kilmer wrote "I think that I shall never see / A poem as lovely as a tree," he wasn't thinking about fishing. Trees and tree limbs are the enemy of the caster. They are immovable obstacles that have been the graveyards of more lures than any other feature of the natural world. I would say avoid fishing around them if it weren't for the fact that fish like to live under tree limbs. Think about it: It is very hard for a hawk or an eagle to dive around a tree limb to snatch a fish. For similar reasons, it is hard for a bear or raccoon to reach in and around underwater tree roots. Fish know this, so you can always find them in the shade of trees or nestled in roots that project underwater. Face it: You are going to have to deal with trees if you don't want to pass up many great fishing spots.

Figure 4-2

One trick you can try is to cast upstream from the tree and then allow your lure to drift under it (or, if there's no current, cast beyond the branch and reel your bait or lure under the tree). While this does the job in many cases, sometime, somewhere, you are going to have to get under that limb in order to have a prayer of catching a completely tantalizing fish.

In that case, having a few different casts at your command is helpful. After you have mastered the overhead cast, you can proceed to the sidearm cast (shown in Figure 4-2). But make sure that you have truly got the overhead cast at your command first; otherwise, you are just kidding yourself. Making two lame casts is rarely better than making no casts at all, and it certainly is worse than making a good overhand cast consistently.

1. The right-handed caster faces the target with left foot slightly forward. (The reverse is true for the left-handed caster in this and the following steps.)

Note that the spool is facing up. The amount of line coming through the tip top is the same as in the overhead cast.

2. Using a short casting stroke, crisply move the rod to the right no more than 90 degrees.

3. Stop the backstroke and begin the forward stroke. As the rod approaches 45 degrees, release thumb pressure.

4. Stop the forward stroke when the rod is in front of you, pointing at the target.

5. As with the overhead cast, begin to apply pressure as the lure nears its target.

Remember to stop the forward stroke when the rod points at the target. If you continue the stroke past this point, your cast will veer way to the left.

Don't try the sidearm cast in a boat with another angler. One day, you may flex too much going forward or backward and drill your companion with some fast-moving treble hooks: not a great way to lay the foundation for a long-term fishing relationship.

Figure 4-3

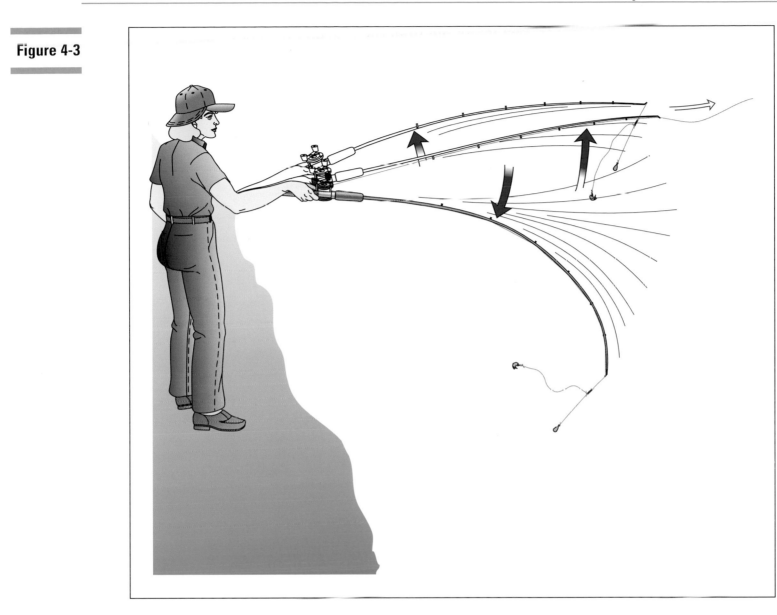

The underhand cast

This is another good cast for getting under obstacles. It is usually more accurate though less powerful than the sidearm cast. I have to confess that when I first saw this cast diagrammed in Al McClane's *New Standard Fishing Encyclopedia*, it looked wrong. Years later, when I had the chance to spend some time with "The Master" (I mean it; McClane was *the greatest* writer and angler), I asked him about this. He demonstrated the cast, and he was right. Again, I urge you to become a good overhead caster before you start to mess with the underhand cast (shown in Figure 4-3). In all casting, remembering to let the rod do the work is important. With this cast, it is critical. If you try "to muscle" or try "to put too much arm" into the cast, it won't work.

Just like the old-fashioned foul shot in basketball, the underhand technique is sweet and accurate.

1. Aim the rod at the target.

For the right-handed caster, the right shoulder points at the target as well (lefties point the other shoulder, etc). Note that the crank handle is pointing upward.

2. Crisply, but not overpoweringly, lift the rod tip to shoulder height.

The weight of the lure flexes the rod tip down.

3. Start the rod's downward stroke, stopping the stroke when your wrist returns to the starting position.

Momentum carries the rod tip downward again, adding even more flex. The rod tip naturally returns to the starting position.

4. Release the spool and point the rod at target in a straight line.

The bend in the rod sends the lure toward the target.

5. Apply thumb pressure to slow down the spool as the lure approaches the target.

Figure 4-4

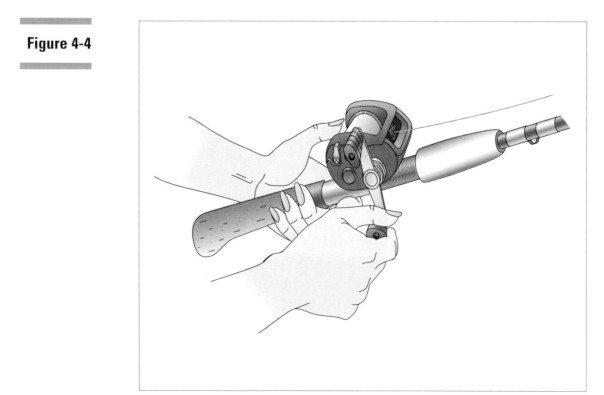

After the Cast

As soon as the lure hits the water, it is time to transfer the rod from your *casting hand* to your *fighting hand*. As shown in Figure 4-4, when a fish strikes, you reel with your right hand and work the rod with your left hand (if you're right-handed).

Your cast may wind up with some slack in the line. You need to retrieve this slack line so that you can strike effectively when a fish hits. If you leave the slack in, a fish may go for your plug, decide it is a phony, and spit it out before you have a chance to drive the hook home. Get rid of the slack. To do this, point your rod tip at your lure or bait. Then grab the line and press it against the shaft of the rod so that some tension is on the line as you reel up, as shown in Figure 4-5. If you don't keep tension on the line, it will coil loosely onto the reel, and you will get a backlash. Actually, I don't know if this is technically a backlash, a frontlash, or just a plain old-fashioned mess. The result, however, is the same: You won't be able to fish until you straighten it out.

Figure 4-5

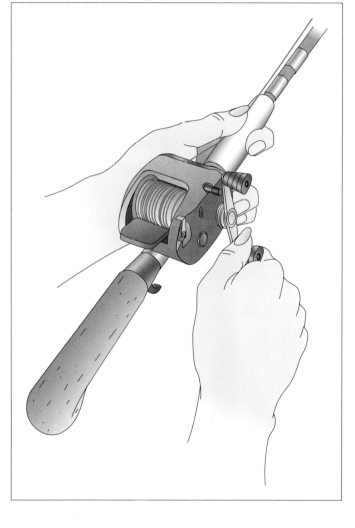

Chapter 5

Spinning and Spin Casting

In This Chapter

Figure 5-1

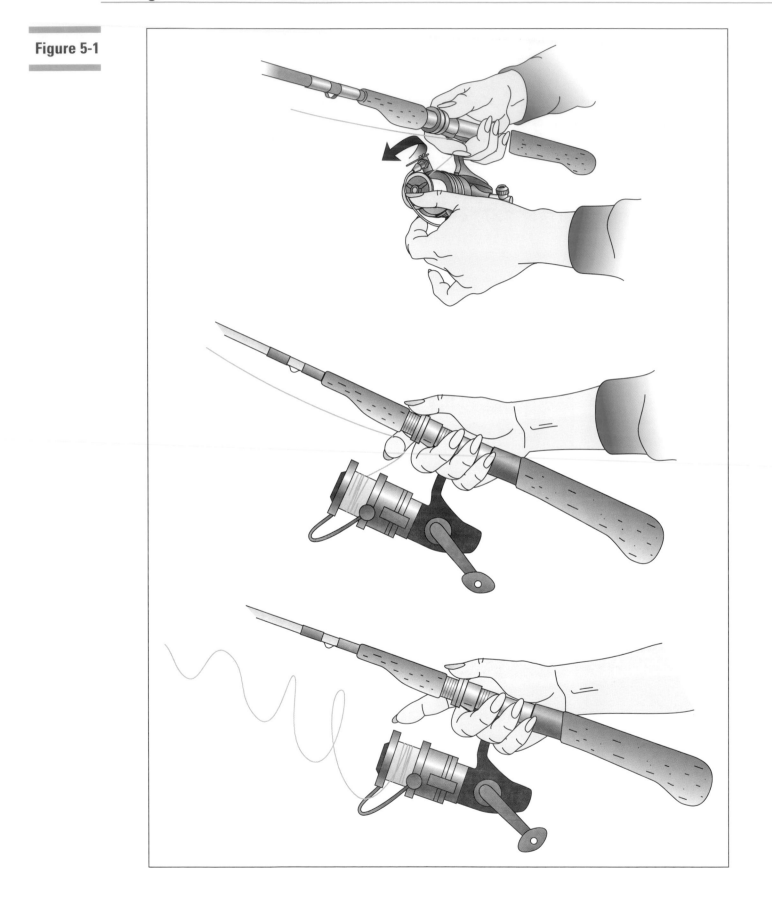

First a Word about Getting Started

I have shown many people how to fish on the mistaken assumption that they know how to *begin* a cast. Most teachers make this same assumption. But if no one ever showed you how to open the bail on your spinning reel and get the line ready for casting, you probably won't figure it out for yourself. It reminds me of the time that I bought my first computer, a big clunky Kaypro that looked like a large lunch box. It came with all kinds of instruction about plugging it in, turning it on, and beginning computing. It also came with a little thing called a *floppy disk* that held the program, but the floppy disk had no diagram to tell me which end of the disk went into the computer first. I guess the Kaypro folks thought that it was self-evident; but I had never seen a floppy disk before and found nothing self-evident about it. So I sat there with a two thousand dollar computer that I couldn't use because I didn't know where to put my $1.98 disk.

So if you are one of those first-timers with a spinning rod, here is how to begin. When you prepare to cast, the reel is on the bottom and the crank (or *handle*) is pointed *away* from your casting arm (as shown in Figure 5-1). To begin the cast, follow these steps:

1. Move the reel's metal arm (or *bail*) over until it clicks into the open position.

Use your free hand to do this.

2. Now, with your casting hand, grip the line with your index finger, holding it against the rod handle under the fleshy party of the first joint.

If you don't hold the line, the weight of the lure will pull too much line off the reel. Also, note that your middle finger should be on the same side of the reel seat as your index finger. You are now ready to cast.

Don't worry if you do forget to open the bail. (We all do it.) The only problem is, the lure isn't going to travel very far if all it has to work with is the few inches of line you've pulled through the tip top.

Figure 5-2

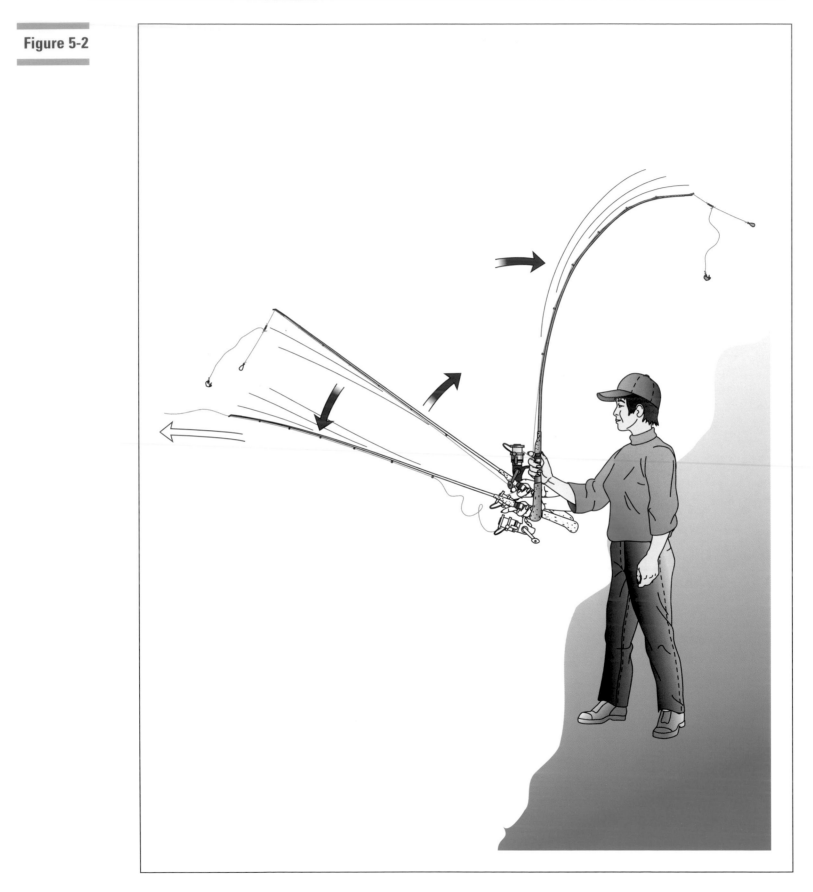

The Overhead Cast

Ninety out of a hundred times, the overhand cast (as shown in Figure 5-2) is the only cast you will use. But even with the more specialized casts, the preparation is pretty much the same.

Follow these steps to complete an overhand cast:

> **1. Pass enough line through the guides so that the rod is slightly flexed by the weight of your bait or lure.**
>
> Usually, use no more than six inches of line for normal freshwater rods and somewhat more line with a surf-casting setup.
>
> **2. If you are right-handed, face the target and position yourself so that your right shoulder points to the target. Lefties point the left shoulder at target.**
>
> **3. Point the rod at the target, open the bail, and secure the line with] your index.**
>
> **4. To begin the cast, position your rod at about 50 degrees.**
>
> **5. Your backstroke should be a crisp (but not overpowering) flick until the rod handle is pointed at 12:00 (that is, directly upright).**
>
> **6. As soon as you reach the 12:00 position, *stop* your backstroke.**
>
> The rod will continue to flex behind you.
>
> **7. As soon as you stop your backstroke, *begin* the forward stroke.**
>
> **8. Release the line, completing your power stroke, when your rod tip is at about 40 degrees (or at about 2:00).**
>
> **9. When the cast reaches the target, press your forefinger against the line on the spool, which stops more line from paying out.**

Most beginners (and quite a few veterans) neglect to use their finger as a brake on the spool. Try this and you will see how much slack develops, all of which you will need to retrieve before you are able to begin fishing. If a strong wind is blowing, you will have a great deal of line to recover if you don't use your forefinger. As you develop a feel for

this technique, you can actually slow down the rate at which line pays out (in much the same way that thumbing will slow down a cast with a bait-casting reel). This technique is called *feathering your cast*. Feathers are light, and mastering this method, therefore, requires a light touch.

Figure 5-3

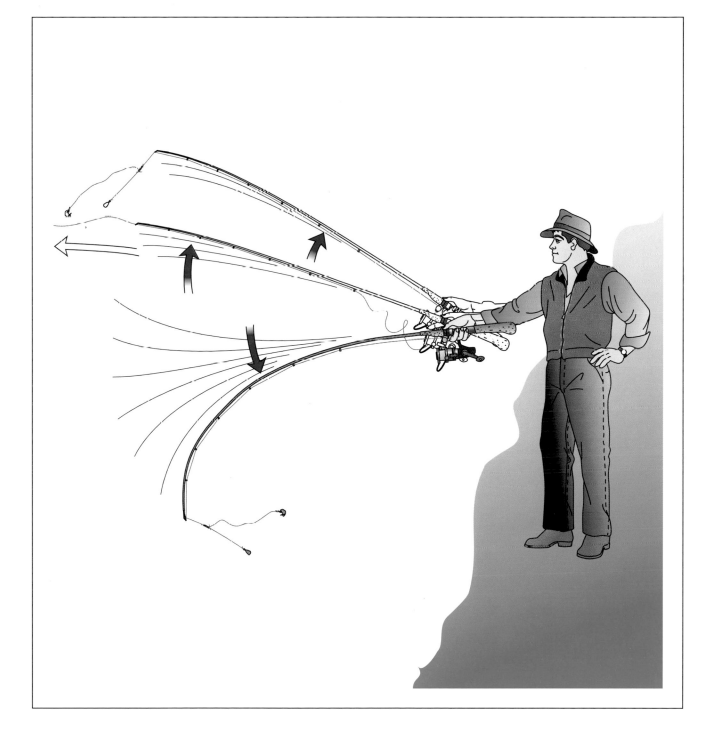

The Underhand Cast

The underhand cast (shown in Figure 5-3) is helpful when you need to sneak that bait or lure under an overhanging limb, beneath a low bridge, and the like. It is for *close-in* work. If you need distance *and* you have to get under something, my advice is to get a boat or to try angling someplace else. However, if you are close to where you want the cast to wind up, then this cast (which has to be executed delicately) will catch you some nice fish that you would otherwise have to pass up.

Follow these steps for the underhand cast:

1. With bail closed, strip line off the reel until the rod is flexed slightly (3 to 6 inches).

2. Face the target, point your casting shoulder at the target, and aim the rod tip straight at the target.

3. Open the bail and secure the line against the rod shaft with your forefinger.

4. Flex your rod by lifting the tip.

This action doesn't require very much power at all.

5. Continue lifting until the rod tip reaches eye level.

6. With just a little more force, push downward; stop your motion when the butt of the rod is back at the starting position.

The tip will continue to flex downward.

7. As the tip begins to return to the starting position, release the line.

8. To stop the line when it reaches the target, press your forefinger against the line paying out of the spool.

Figure 5-4

The Sidearm Cast

Sometimes you see a nice fish, and the only possible way to cast to it is with a sidearm motion (shown in Figure 5-4). Maybe the day is too windy, or an overhang prevents an overhead cast. Maybe some underbrush prevents an underhand cast. As with the underarm cast, this maneuver is one that you will only perfect when you truly understand that the rod has to do the work for you. Muscle this cast, and you will end up casting way off target.

Follow these steps for the sidearm cast:

1. Strip off just enough line to flex the rod slightly (3 to 6 inches).

2. Face the target. Righties, put your left foot slightly forward. (Lefties, put the right foot forward.)

3. At belt level, point your rod at the target, open the bail, and secure the line with your forefinger.

4. Righties should move the rod with an easy stroke to the right about 45 degrees. (Lefties should move the rod left 45 degrees.)

5. Snap the rod back crisply to the starting position.

6. As the rod tip begins to point more to the front than it does to the side, release the line (which was held down by your forefinger).

7. Point the rod straight at the target and stop the line with your forefinger as the lure or bait reaches the target.

As you did with the underhand cast, strive for an easy motion, and just let the flexing of the rod do the work. Understatement (or *undercastment*, if that's a word) is what you want here. This cast is a good one to have in your arsenal, but it is not one you want to perfect in an actual fishing situation. Do it on the lawn until you have it down. And beginners, don't do this in a boat with a friend (even if you don't like the friend very much).

Figure 5-5

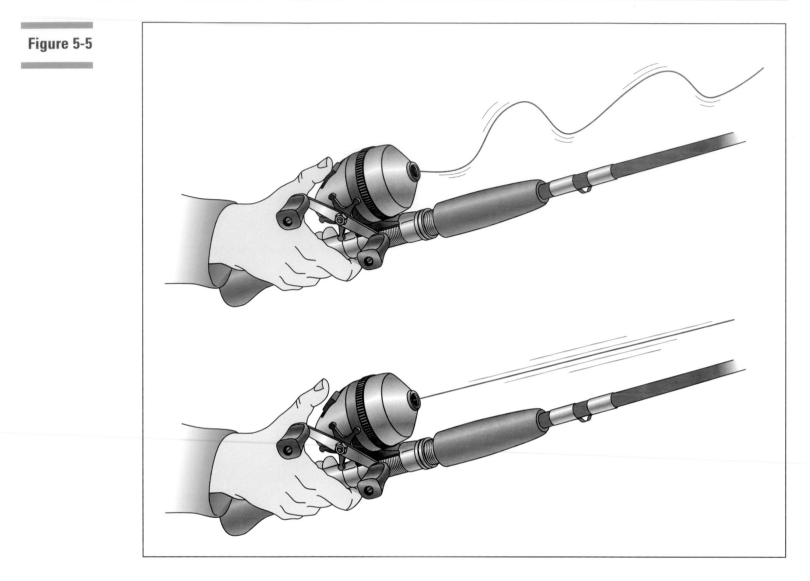

Spin Casting

Spin casting is the least "mess-up-able" method of casting with a rod and reel. The main heartbreak that it avoids is backlash. Still, you do have to cast. The actual cast is executed like the casts with the spinning reel. The difference is that the reel is positioned on top of the rod, as with bait casting. This is to accommodate your thumb on the push button at the bottom of the spin-casting reel. Otherwise, the physics of the cast is the same as spinning: Where you are instructed to release line in a classic spinning cast, you simply depress the button on a spin-casting outfit. When you want to stop the line from paying out, release the button (as shown in Figure 5-5).

Oops! It Went Too Far and Wrapped Around a Branch!

Successful fishing is often a game of inches. Come to think of it, what sport isn't? A curve ball on the outside corner, a forward pass between two defenders, a drive over a bunker — these skills require accuracy, too. The same goes with fishing. So if you want to get your cast in there where the fish are, you are going to miss by inches and hang up from time to time. Everybody does. With care, you will do it less, but you are still going to do it. Sometimes you can also undo it.

The most common hang-up involves wrapping your line around a branch. The natural reaction here is usually a three-act play:

ACT I: You realize your mistake as the lure starts to overshoot the target.

ACT II: You say "Oh, shoot!" and instinctively recoil.

ACT III: The lure snugs up against the branch, often adding a knot to your troubles.

Restrain yourself. Don't pull back on the rod. When your lure wraps around a branch, the damage is done, and pulling is not going to undo it. (It will only make the situation worse.) Sometimes, if you do nothing, the line will wrap, and then, as it comes to a sudden halt, the momentum of the cast causes the lure to recoil and unwind all by itself. (This happens more times than it doesn't when fishing a plastic worm with the hook embedded in it.) If you have come this far and you are lucky, you now have a hook and line draped over a tree limb. Here's what to do next:

1. Point your rod at the hook.

2. Very gently, reel up any slack until you come tight.

3. By reeling slowly and gently and just nudging the rod tip, you can often coax the hook over the limb, thereby freeing it.

4. Retrieve your lure normally.

Sometimes, the resulting *kerplunk* of the lure on the water makes for a more natural landing than a well-executed cast, and the reward can be a fish.

I wouldn't be doing my job if I left you thinking that every bad cast can be undone by keeping a cool head and using an unsnagging trick like this. While it may work, it doesn't always work. Face it: You are going to lose line and gear at least some of the time.

While I'm on the Subject of Hang-ups

TIP

Tree branches aren't the only lure-and-line stealers. You can hang up on underwater rocks (or *any* submerged obstacle). And as with catching fish, a number of techniques and strategies (including a couple of important *don'ts*) apply:

- Don't rear back with your rod and put a lot of pressure on it, and don't jerk it either. You will break a rod one of these days (which is a big price to pay, even if the alternative is losing an expensive lure).

- If firm (but not overpowering) pressure won't free a snagged line, I often put the rod down and strip some more line off. Then I wrap the line around my hands a couple of times and pull straight on the line, being careful that I don't let the line cut into my hands. Usually, if the hook has any chance of breaking free, this does the trick.

SAFETY

- This wrap-and-pull technique is good for underwater obstacles, particularly the kind you run into off the beach. Don't try this method if the hang-up is in a tree. You can slingshot a lure out of a tree with tremendous force, and chances are you will be looking straight down the line at your lure. Guess what path that lure is going to take as it hurtles out of the brush — right at your face!

- If you are in a stream, sometimes walking downstream to see if changing the angle of pressure will free the hook is helpful. If you can't get downstream (if the stream is too deep, or if the current is too swift), I have seen anglers put a bobber on the line and then let the bobber float downstream. This trick can have the effect of exerting some downstream pressure as you reel in.

- The final decision is to "fish or cut bait," as the saying goes. In this case, it can also mean cutting line, lures, flies, and the like. After trying to rescue your equipment for a while, you need to consider the following: You wait all week to try and get in a little fishing. When you get right down to it, you don't spend all that much time actually fishing, even when you do get the time. Getting rigged up, in and out of waders, in and out of boats, and the like eats up a great deal of time. How much time do you want to spend trying to save a lure or bait? Sometimes the answer is "give up and get back to fishing!" You will be amazed at how good you will feel as soon as you catch a fish.

Chapter 6

How to Strike, Fight, and Land (and Sometimes Release) Fish

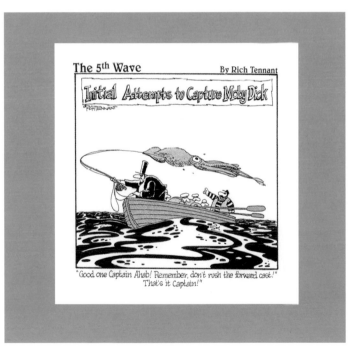

In This Chapter

▸ Striking a fish

▸ Catching a fish

▸ Fighting a fish

▸ Landing or boating a fish

▸ Releasing a fish

Should I Strike Now?

Different fish have different takes. Whereas a pike may slaughter your topwater bait, a trout may approach your fly in a daintier fashion. A bass may play with a lure. A bluefish may slam it. Some fish will take surface lures with wild abandon, yet be much more deliberate with a subsurface bait. The general rule is this: There is no *one* general rule for when to strike. To be an effective angler, you need to know your fish and its behavior.

A savage strike doesn't require a savage response from the angler. Usually, all this sort of response does is ensure that you pull your bait, lure, or fly away from the fish before you have a chance to set the hook. You need to come tight to the fish: All the slack must be gone from your line, and you must feel the weight of the fish *before* you drive the hook home.

Some fish, like the tarpon, require a couple of good, slamming strikes at this point. The trout, on the other hand, needs just a slight jerk to set the hook. With bass and pike that tend to play with the bait, you need to let them run with it for a bit. To get one securely on your hook, follow these steps:

1. **Drop the rod tip when you feel the fish take your lure or bait.**

2. **After giving the fish a little while to get the bait inside its mouth, point the rod at the fish, reel in as you drop your rod tip until you have taken up all the slack, and then lift the rod forcefully to set the hook.**

3. **Give the fish a good firm whack by lifting the rod high.**

   If you have a stiff rod with a fast tip, your fish should be on at this point.

4. **Whack it again for good measure — maybe twice more.**

Soft rods require even more forcefulness in the hook-setting motion. Some rods, although they are nice, safe casters, are too soft ever to set the hook. If you follow all of these recommendations and just can't seem to set a hook, you may need a rod with a faster tip.

Catching a Fish, or "Jeepers, It's On! Now What Do I Do?"

Having a fish on the end of your line is like any other emergency situation: If you have never been through it before, you may lose your head. Remember this piece of advice: It's an emergency for the fish, not for you. If you maintain your cool, you can win this fight. Millions of anglers have done it before you, so it isn't magic. Still, you do need to know what you are doing. Fighting and beating fish is one art where I promise you that you can learn from your mistakes because you will replay them a thousand times in your head. The better the fish, the more times you will tell yourself, "Gee, if only I'd. . . ."

And then, after you finally learn how to fight your average fish, you will hook into a big one someday, and it's a whole new ball game (with a whole *new* set of mistakes to make and learn from).

Fighting: This Is the Fun Part

Having a fish on and not knowing what to do can be a source of much anxiety. It shouldn't be. Having a fish on is the fun part of fishing. That tug. That pushing and head-shaking and throbbing. That wildness. These are the prime thrills of fishing. It's you against the fish, and the fish is in its element. That you will win is not a foregone conclusion (although the more fish you fight, the better your chances are). Win or lose, the fight is always a thrill. Learn to savor it.

Remember that your rod is your buddy

A good fishing rod can be a great tool *if* you remember to let it help you fight the fish. Let the rod do some of the work. It was designed to do just that. Follow the advice of Izaak Walton and keep the fish under the bend of the rod. This means that you should be holding the rod at an angle that allows it to bend. It doesn't have to bend double, but it has to bend. This flexing of the rod, more than anything else, will tire (and eventually conquer) a fish. No matter how far the fish runs, no matter how much it jumps or shakes, the rod will flex, putting pressure on the hook, which is buried in its flesh.

The reel is working for you, too

When fighting a fish, the drag mechanism on your reel is another potential ally. If you have set the drag properly, the drag acts as a brake mechanism that can further tire the fish. In most cases, the time to set the drag is before you cast. Adjusting the drag while you are fishing becomes just one more thing that you can mess up, and I don't recommend doing it.

The exception is when you are fighting a big fish in saltwater. In this case, the specially designed drag can be adjusted at certain times during the fight. My advice is this: Don't do anything unless someone with a great deal more experience than you tells you to do it. Because different kinds of fish fight differently, remember, in setting the drag, to make the punishment fit the crime. For example, a big bluefish requires more pre-set drag than a medium weakfish. Also bear in mind that drag increases the resistance working against the fish — it doesn't stop it dead in its tracks. The purpose of drag is to *tire* the fish.

Even the line is an ally

When a large fish runs off a great deal of line, the resistance of the water against the line creates even more drag. This can work in your favor if you have a sense of how much added pressure your tackle can take. Only practice will teach you this lesson.

Heads up

Heads up means that the head of the fish points up. If you are able to keep the head of the fish up, *you* are directing the fight. With its head up, the fish is disoriented and bewildered and can't see where to go (that is, it can't see a rock to slip under or a weed bed to dive for). If the fish can get its head down, you are in the position of reacting while the fish picks where it will take the fight.

Keeping the head up doesn't mean rearing back at all costs. Sometimes a little pressure to the side or from side to side will do the trick. You are in contact with the fish, and you just have to feel your way through the fight, responding to its twists and turns by pulling back, easing up, or changing direction — whatever it takes.

Let the current help you

A fish is going to run away from the pressure of hook, line, and rod. If you have hooked your fish in moving water, try to position yourself downstream from the fish. That way, the fish is not only fighting you and your tackle, it is also fighting the current. This move may not always be possible, but when it is, do it, even if you have to back out of the stream and walk downstream.

He went in the weeds: I lose

If the fish burrows into the weeds, you may well have lost it, but not always. True, if you bend the rod every which way trying to get the fish out of the weeds, you will probably break off sooner or later. However, if you point your rod tip straight at the fish, reel up tight, and start walking backwards, you may coax the fish out of the weeds.

Jumping

People are always telling us not to jump to conclusions. I won't pass judgment on the non-angling side of life, but if your tussle with a fish *concludes* on a jump, it can mean only one thing — the fish has jumped free, and your fight is over. It may have broken the line or shaken the hook, but either way, it's off. In most such cases, I bow (drop my rod tip) when a fish jumps. When I bow to a fish, I literally bow. I bend from the waist, drop my rod tip, and extend my arms like a waiter offering a tray full of canapes. As soon as the fish falls back to the water, I come tight again. When a fish is airborne, it may reach a point in its trajectory when all of its weight and momentum snap against the line. Without the buoyancy of the water to act as a shock absorber, this is a very good time for knots to break under the added force of gravity. A hard-mouthed fish, like a tarpon, may not be very deeply hooked to begin with. The force of a jump may be all that is needed to dislodge a hook.

Figure 6-1

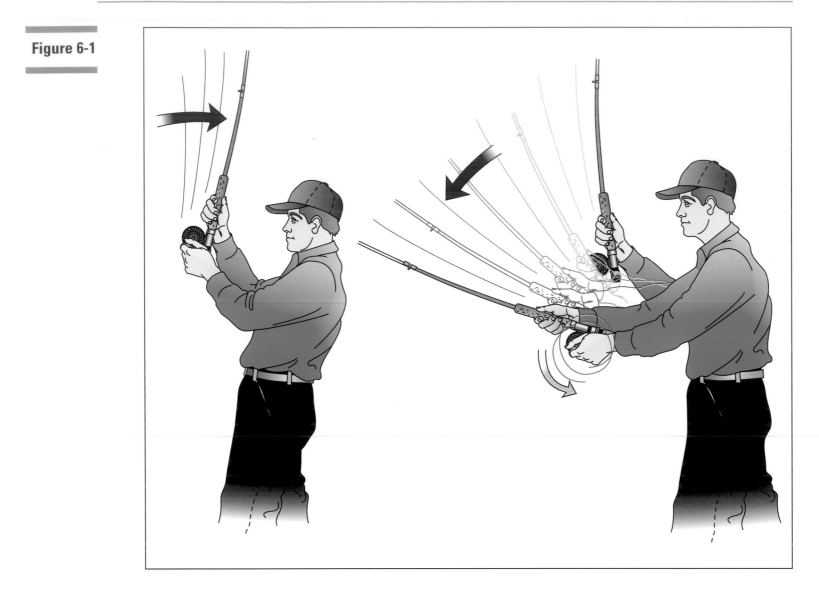

Pull up, reel down

When fighting a fish, the idea is to tire the fish and to recover line that the fish has taken off the reel so that you can eventually get the fish close enough to grasp or gaff. The reeling up is the longest and most tiring part of the fight, and it's one that doesn't come naturally.

The wrong way

Most newcomers get a fish on and reel for dear life. This technique will do you no good. It can even do you harm by causing bad line twist.

The right way

As indicated in Figure 6-1, *pull up* to try to bring the fish toward you; then drop the rod tip and, as you do, reel up line. Remember: As you reel in, drop the rod tip so that you have some place to go when you pull up again.

Remember, too, that every pull up is not going to bring the fish in. Sometimes a fish will take a lot of line before you are able to recover any. Or you may have gained a great deal of line, and then the fish sees the boat and tears away on another run. Keep the pressure on — it's the only way to land the fish. Don't fiddle with the drag because, more often than not, doing so puts too much pressure on your tackle, and I can almost guarantee that you will lose the fish.

Playing the fish

You should always try to get the fish in as soon as possible, especially if you are going to release it. The longer the fish fights, the more lactic acid it builds up, and the harder it is to revive. Releasing (letting go of) a fish that you have fought to the point of exhaustion before you have spent the time to revive it often makes no sense because the fish may well die anyway.

In the ocean, ending the fight quickly is even more important (even if you are keeping the fish) because a long, splashy fight is a great way to attract a predator (like a shark) who will end the fight for you as he takes a meal. This happened to me in the Florida Keys with a tarpon that weighed well over 100 pounds. I fought hard, but I could have fought harder and followed my guide's advice and have gotten the tarpon into the boat within ten minutes. Instead, I prolonged the fight, and my heart was broken as, two hundred yards out, I saw a tremendous commotion and then felt my line grow slack as a huge shark devoured my tarpon.

Light tackle equals a longer fight

While it is more sporty to subdue fish on lighter tackle, you need to use enough tackle to do the job. Using an outfit that doesn't let you bear down on the fish may still land you a fish after a long fight; but if the fish is totally exhausted when you land it, you didn't use heavy enough gear, or you didn't push your gear to the limit.

Figure 6-2

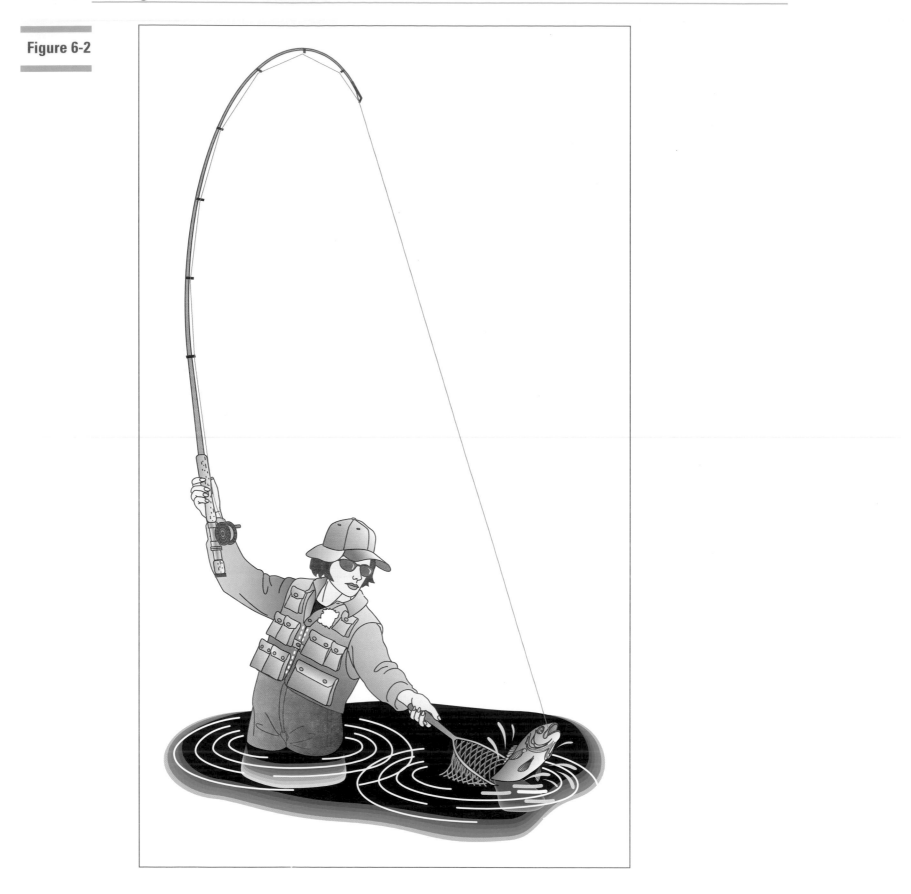

Landing or Boating the Fish

After you have subdued a fish, your next task is to land it or boat it. This section gives you the lay of the land (or the water) for most fish that you can land by yourself. I am going to assume that if you are going for big game, you either already know what to do or will be fishing with a guide or someone with experience. Landing a big fish is not something to do on your own with only a book as your guide, unless you are a real dummy. (It's a word my publishers asked me to avoid in this book, but I can't think of another word to describe someone who tussles with a big and dangerous game fish without actual physical help and personal experience.)

Do I need a net?

For trout and bass, "the experts" say that you definitely should have a net if you want to release fish back into the water in the hopes that they will live and reproduce. The theory behind this reasoning is that, if you use a net, the fish will be less exhausted when netted rather than landed by hand.

Having said that, I can tell you that I rarely use a net when trout fishing (or when bass fishing, for that matter). I find, at this stage of my angling career, that I can get most fish within my grasp when they still have some life in them. With trout, I reach under the belly and lift up until I am cradling the fish gently. Then I lift it out of the water. For bass, I grab the fish by the lower lip. If I am fishing a lure that has several treble hooks, I hold the line taut with my free hand and then come around with my rod hand to grasp the fish by the lower lip. If I have a really big fish, I use a net. You may want to use a net for all fish, and that's perfectly fine.

If you use a net, you should flip it over so that it is hanging in front of you as the fight concludes. Make sure the net is wet, so that you do not damage the protective mucous-like slime that coats the fish. As shown in Figure 6-2, hold the rod tip high and slip the net over the fish, tail first. Remember to keep the fish in the water until you have the net around it.

Before you catch (or release)

If you intend to release a fish, you should follow these few rules:

- Make up your mind whether to catch or release when you set the hook.

- Try to set the hook quickly so the fish cannot swallow it too deeply.

- Minimize the time of the fight. (An exhausted fish is not a strong candidate for survival.)

- Consider using barbless hooks.

After the fish is landed or boated

These tips increase a fish's chances of surviving:

- Leave the fish in the water as much as possible.

- Handle the fish as little as possible.

  Use forceps or pliers to remove the hook.

- Use a wet rag (if you have one handy) to hold the fish. (This technique causes less damage to its scales and protective coating.)

- Wet your hands before handling the fish.

- If the hook is very deep inside the fish's mouth, cut off the leader. In many cases, the hook will eventually rust out or work itself free. By the way, artificials are usually not taken deep.

Releasing a fish

Sometimes, releasing the fish is relatively easy. You simply remove the hook and the fish wiggles vigorously, which lets you know that it is ready to take off for freedom. Sometimes, the fish won't wait for you to release it. Instead, it will wriggle free and high-tail it.

Often, however, the fish is totally exhausted. If you simply released it right away, you would have a belly-up, soon-to-be-dead fish on your hands. Before you *release*, you need to *revive*.

A good rule of thumb to follow in figuring out if a fish needs reviving is this: If the fish lets you hold it and doesn't struggle, revive it. After all, any self-respecting wild animal will take off likc greased lightning to escape the clutches of a strange creature. To a fish, a human is a strange creature.

Reviving a fish

Follow these steps (illustrated in Figure 6-3) to help ensure that a caught-and-released fish survives:

1. Hold the fish gently and keep it under the surface of the water.

Cradle it from below if you can. If you cannot, hold it gently by its sides. You may grasp some mid-size fish (salmon and stripers, for example) by the tail.

2. If you are in heavy current, move to gentler current.

3. Point the fish upstream.
On lakes or in the ocean, however, current usually isn't a factor when reviving a fish.

4. Move the fish backward and forward so that its gills are forced to open and close.

When properly done, this technique delivers oxygen to a heavily oxygen-depleted fish. Reviving the fish so that it can swim under its own steam may take a few minutes. It lets you know that it is ready to be released when it starts to wiggle.

5. Release the fish.

It should swim slowly away. If it rolls over on its back and lays there, this is not a good sign. Bring the fish back under your control and continue to revive it.

Figure 6-3

Chapter 7

Where and When to Fish

In This Chapter

▶ The right places
▶ The right times

Figure 7-1

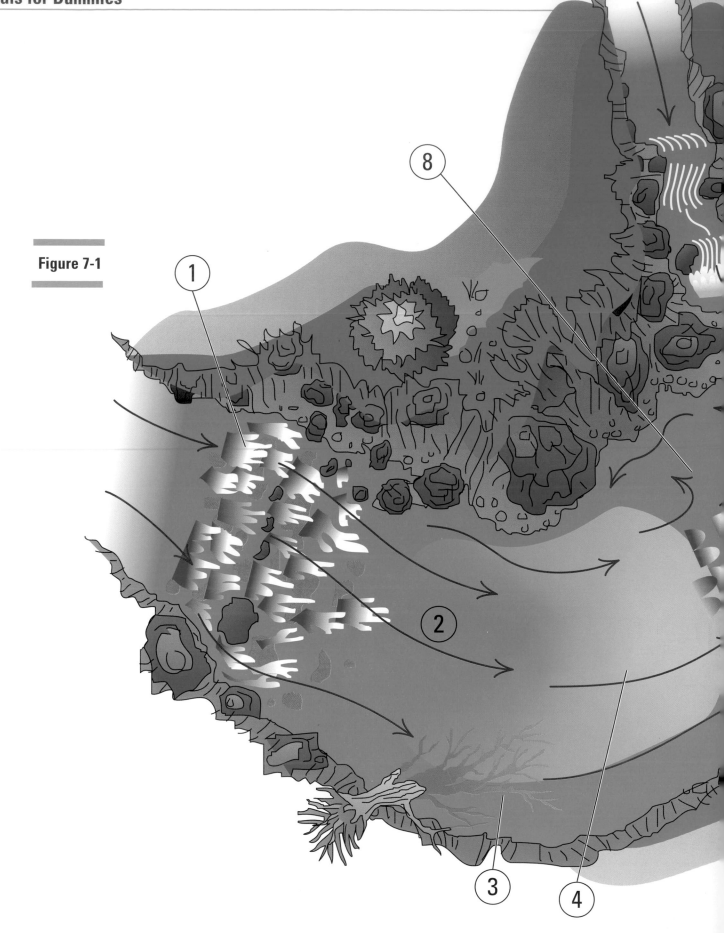

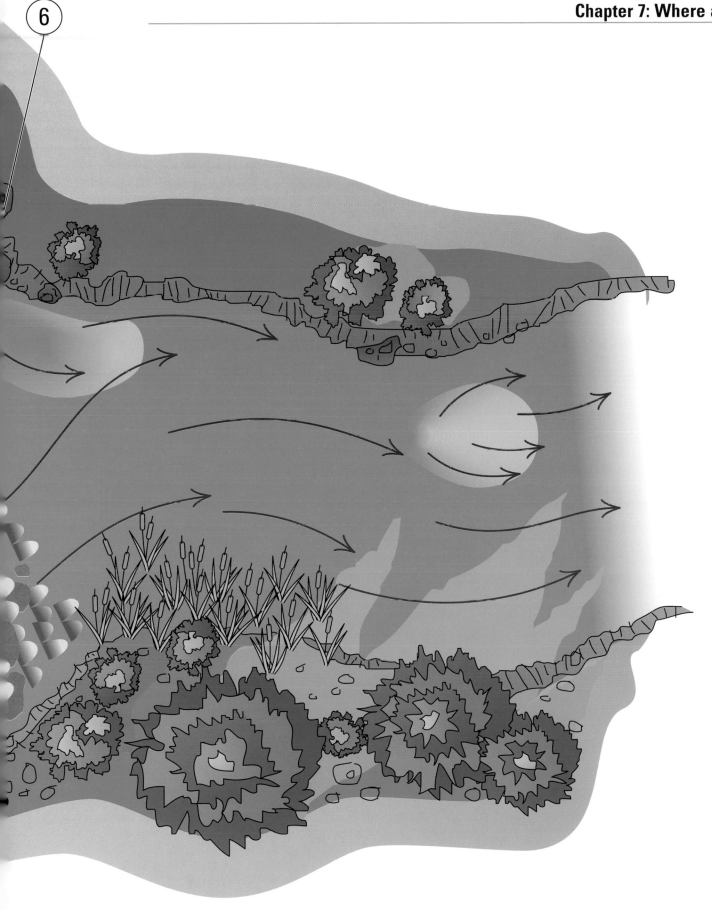

Where

All animals that hunt — whether they are lions, humans, or striped bass — hunt the zone known as *the edge*. It could be where deep water rises to shallow, where fast current meets slow, or where grassland meets water hole. It is the place where prey lose their caution and temporarily leave the safety of their lairs to pursue food (or sometimes mate). Prey often perform these activities to the point of not being tuned into dangers. Predators lie in wait until their prey is thus exposed, and then they strike.

As an angler, or predator, you seek out your prey in those areas where they forsake security in pursuit of their basic drives. The more food around for your prey, the easier it is for you to approach.

Whatever fish you fish for and however you choose to fish, the principles in this little drama are repeated over and over without fail: The angler offers something that looks like safe food to the fish. Fish bites. Angler hooks fish.

Rivers and streams

The basic fact of life in a river or stream is moving water. Food is carried along by the current. Bait fish dart out into the current while seeking bugs, worms, and the like. Game fish move out into the current to eat the same things the bait fish eat (and they eat the bait fish, too). You should look for those places where predators can hang out in security but which are also close to the food being carried on the watery conveyor belt of the stream.

Riffle, pool, riffle

A normal free-stone river (*free-stone*, by the way, means what it says: a river with a great number of stones lying around) is made up of two areas:

- **Riffles:** Rocky areas with fast-moving water

- **Pools:** Deeper areas where the current slows

In trying to visualize a free stone stream, think of a typical mountain stream with boulders and rocks.

The other kind of stream is the *spring creek*, which as its name implies, rises from a subterranean source. It is usually more gentle and slow-moving than a free-stone river and it usually has weed beds and undercut banks.

As illustrated in Figure 7-1, a typical riffle pool system has a number of likely places for game fish, particularly bass and trout.

1. The riffle. In the riffle, rocks break up the current flow. Water picks up more oxygen from this turbulence and provides a rich habitat ground for insects and other aquatic life. Game fish hang out in the lee of the current, behind or directly in front of rocks or at the margins of the stream bed, where the current slows and undercut banks may offer shelter. In these conditions, with food zipping by, fish tend to strike quickly at anything that looks like food. Flyrodders want bushy, very floatworthy flies. Exact imitation is not as important as it is in slower water.

2. The head of the pool. As the current rushes into the head of the pool, it often digs a nice hole. Fish will hold in the depths and rise to take the food which flows through the funnel that characterizes the entry to many pools in a classic riffle pool system. Typically the current will enter in a V-shape. At the outside edges of the V, you can also prospect for fish. (They often show themselves as they feed on floating food.)

3. Deadfalls, logs, rocks, debris. Anything that obstructs the current offers a place for a predator to lie in wait.

4. The middle of the pool. This is usually the place where the current is slowest. In many rivers, it is also the place where the fishing is the slowest. You will occasionally find big fish in this part of the pool; but for the most part, little current means little edge (which means not-so-great fishing). If the current is clipping along, however, try your luck in this area. Hey, you never know.

5. Weed beds. These are usually found in slower streams and spring creeks. Weeds offer shelter, and they are often rich in fish food, such as freshwater shrimp and insects of all types. Predator fish hang out in or near weeds because such a location is conveniently close to their food supply.

6. Tributaries. Where water from a smaller stream enters a larger stream, it is usually cooler and more oxygen rich. You may well find game fish just down stream of the outlet of a feeder stream (the place where a tributary flows into a larger body of water). As far as those fish are concerned, they are at the head of a pool.

7. Spring holes. Subsurface springs beneath rivers and creeks bring cool water in the hot weather and warmer water in the cold weather. Often, the water temperature of a spring is close to the optimum for fish activity. Wherever you find an underwater spring, you may find nice fish. How do you know where a subsurface spring is? Someone tells you, or you figure it out after fishing a particular stretch of stream in all conditions. Say it's the middle of a heat wave in the summer, and you catch a few fish at a particular spot in the depths of a pool. The odds are you have hit upon the location of a spring hole. Mark it and remember it next year when heat strikes again.

8. Eddies. The *hydrodynamics* of some pools — that is, the physics of the water flow as it interacts with the structure of the pool — creates calm areas that collect many of the dead insects and shellfish that float downstream. The pickings are easy, so in the case of trout, you will see very gentle feeding activity. A delicate casting hand and a quiet approach can reward you with nice fish.

9. Shade. Bankside trees offer shade, a thing that fish seek on bright sunny days. Shade also offers fish some protection from the view of predatory hawks, eagles, and ospreys.

Bankside trees and shrubs offer rich habitat for all kinds of insects. Aquatic insects hatch out of the water and often spend a day or two in the trees and shrubs before returning to mate over the water. So if you see mayflies in the shrubs during the day, look for a spinner fall nearby at night. Also, trees and bushes that are in bloom attract nonaquatic insects that some-times find their way into the water.

Catastrophic drift — far from a catastrophe

Sometimes the insect or shellfish population can outgrow the capacity of a particular weed bed. When this happens, whole battalions of little organisms abandon their native weed pocket and take to the current in search of new food. This activity is known as *catastrophic drift.* If this happens while you are on the stream, you will be treated to a major feeding frenzy. The upside is that the fish are feeding like crazy. The downside is, with so much food in the water, the odds aren't great they will take whatever you are throwing at them. Still, a feeding frenzy brought about by catastrophic drift provides a unique fishing opportunity.

10. The tail. As the water leaves the pool to enter another riffle, it often shallows out and gets very glassy and slick. When a great deal of insect activity takes place, game fish often venture into this shallow water and slash about. These circumstances provide for tricky fishing, and the fish can be spooky (but exciting in a special way). I can't really describe this situation other than to say that the water looks pregnant with the possibility of good fishing.

Taking on a big river

The first time you step into a huge river like the Yellowstone, you will find so much fishy looking water that you really won't know where to start. I have found that the best thing to do in these cases is to think of a really big river as a bunch of smaller rivers.

- If there is an island in the middle of a big river, treat each channel as if it were a separate smaller river.

- Treat the island as if it were a big rock in the middle of a stream. Fish will hang just upstream and just downstream of the island, where there is some protection from the current.

- If you are fishing from the bank and a current line (the edge of the current) is about 20 feet out from the bank, fish the 20 feet of river between the current and the bank as a separate stream.

By breaking the big problem down into separate parts, you can tackle the task at hand in manageable bites.

Dead water: don't waste your time

When fishing a lazy river with big bends and slow deep pools (the Delaware River in New York State is one such river and almost any Ozark stream would be another), remember that trout and bass concentrate in areas where there is some current. Those long, slow, mid-pool stretches look like inviting spots to fish, but nine times out of ten — make that ninety-nine million times out of ninety-nine million and one — you will not catch anything in this kind of water. If you are floating downstream in a boat or canoe, pass by such a pool and save your casting for water that fits the fish-holding profile. (Unless, of course, you see a fish.)

Lakes and reservoirs

Lakes and reservoirs are both standing bodies of water with a few important differences.

- A reservoir is a more recent creation than a lake. (After all, most lakes have been around since the last Ice Age, but reservoirs are man-made and are relatively recent creations.) Reservoirs haven't had time to evolve all the subtle habitat features of a good old-fashioned lake.

- Reservoirs can have their level raised or lowered and are, therefore, subject to tremendous fluctuations in depth. Not only does this fluctuation have the obvious effect of determining how much water is available for the fish to hang out in, it also means that significant parts of the reservoir bottom can dry out in periods of low water, affecting the long-term survival of shallow-water bait fish, insects, shellfish, and aquatic vegetation.

A promise from the author (and a picture, too)

I promise that I won't give you a diagram full of little fish marks and 30 different kinds of structures to look for. If you have ever read a how-to fishing book before, you know what I am talking about. "Fish for walleye on drop-offs. Try bass over gravely bottoms. Look for northerns by weedy shores." Such suggestions are all true; but collectively, they are a big chunk to swallow in one gulp.

It's much better, I think, to remember the idea of *the edge* (mentioned earlier in this chapter in the section titled "Where"). Look for current, changes in depth, shelter, or anything that breaks up the uniform character of the water. When you discover an edge, realize that game fish and bait fish have to deal with it in various ways. Some fish feed on one side of it. Some lurk on the other side.

I guess this whole concept does require a picture after all, but I'll keep it simple. Figure 7-2 represents a lake that exists nowhere but in a fishing book. It has a little bit of everything that you might find in any lake from the Arctic Circle to Patagonia.

Figure 7-2

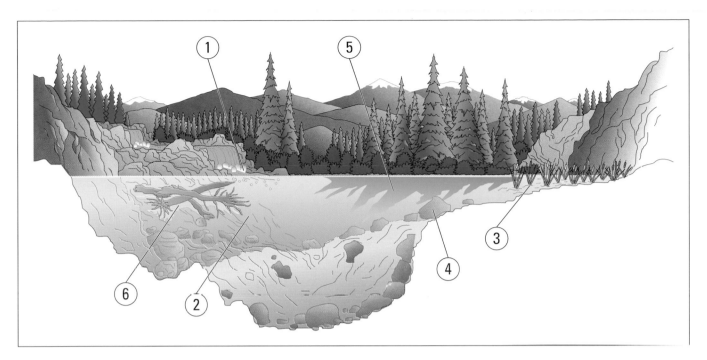

1. Inlets and outlets: Wherever water flows into or out of a lake, bait follows, and game fish concentrate to feed.

2. Drop-offs: Wherever the structure goes from shallow to deeper, you may find game fish lurking in water that is in a comfortable temperature zone. This usually puts game fish *under* bait fish (which they can ambush from below).

3. Weed beds: Weeds can be a haven for bait fish, a breeding ground for crus taceans and insects, and (because of these assets) a magnet for game fish. Weed beds also offer a place for game fish to hide from prey and predators.

4. Rocky points: Rocky points can block the wind, divert a current, and offer shade. In other words, rocky points provide classic edges.

5. Shade: Trees on the banks and lily pads in the shallows offer shade (which affects water temperature). Shade affects the view of dangerous predators, like herons and raccoons, and that limits their ability to prey on game fish.

6. Underwater stuff: Sunken islands, drowned trees, and fallen trees offer structure, which translates into hiding places for predators and habitat for bait.

Birds

Feeding birds are always a sign that bait is available — whether it is in the form of insects or bait fish. This situation is a no-brainer. Fish where the birds are.

Other bird signs are more subtle. For example, a blue heron (or any other wading bird that is known to feed on bait fish) is a promising sign for anglers. If you see such a bird hanging around the same pool day after day, chances are that Mr. Heron knows that this pool is a regular food source. (You can count on Mr. Game Fish to have reached the same conclusion.)

Deep thoughts

"How deep should I fish?" This is a question that only the fish can answer. Obviously, you need to fish where the fish are. Water temperature has a great deal to do with their location. If you can figure out where the water is at the optimum temperature level, that's a good place to start fishing. Some electronic devices take the water temperature at various depths, but (as with all electronic devices) they cost money.

A do-it-yourself temperature gauge

You don't always need a sophisticated gauge for reading temperatures at different depths. Say you want to find out what the temperature is at ten feet. Here's a simple way to do that:

> **1. Tie an inexpensive (but accurate) outdoor thermometer to the end of a line.**
>
> **2. Let out ten feet of line (you can guesstimate this) and attach a bobber to the line at the ten-foot point.**
>
> **3. Then put the thermometer in the water, let the thermometer sink, and take a reading.**

To check the temperature at other depths, just let out five more feet of line (for example), move the bobber five feet up the line, and you get a fifteen foot reading, and so on.

Forget about the deep blue sea

If you fish on the ocean, chances are that you won't start by venturing out 10, 20, or 100 miles to blue water all on your own. For one thing, the exorbitant cost of a boat and gear for this type of fishing is beyond the reach of most beginning anglers — make that most anglers, including yours truly. Most of your fishing will be done closer to shore in shallower water (less than a hundred feet of depth). When you narrow your search field down to this strip of shallow coastal waters, the overwhelmingly big ocean begins to take on the characteristics of a combination of river and lake.

It's like robbing a bank

When the notorious stick-up man, Willie Sutton, was asked why he robbed banks, he gave a sensible answer: "Because that's where the money is." If you want to catch fish, go where the bait is. Think of the ocean as a bank filled not with money but with bait. Just as when fishing in a stream or lake, the first thing to look for is feeding fish. The second thing to look for is bait. And the third thing to look for (actually it's two things) is current and structure.

Tides are the key

Anyone with any ocean angling experience knows that tides are critically important. There are two high tides and two low tides each day. For the angler, this means roughly dividing the day into six hours of incoming water and six hours of outgoing water (followed by six more hours of incoming water and six more hours of outgoing water). When the tide is moving, you will find a current coming in and out of creeks, back bays, and the like. Treat this current just as you would treat a river or stream, and fish the moving tide accordingly. If a current sweeps by a rocky outcropping, look for fish just as if they were holding behind a subsurface rock in a trout stream.

Here are some additional tidal tips:

- Try to fish when the tide is moving. At slack tide — in other words, still water at the end of a tide — there is very little action that would cause bait to concentrate. Consequently there is nothing to concentrate game fish.

- On an outgoing tide, position yourself just outside creek mouths, bay mouths, and harbor mouths. That is where the bait (and the fish) will be as the tide recedes.

- On an incoming tide, you will often find fish just inside of bay and harbor mouths. Most anglers, however, find this situation to be less of a sure bet than finding fish on an outgoing tide.

- At low tide, examine exposed flats to see the contours of the bottom. You will find holes, troughs, and subsurface structure to check out later during high tide.

- When fishing shallow flats, the incoming tide will often bring nice fish out of deeper water as they follow bait onto the flats.

- As in stream fishing, structure attracts game fish. At high tide, try rocky jetties that attract fish to nooks and crannies.

- Be mindful of the phase of the moon. The full moon will bring abnormally high and low tides. This situation will affect ocean access and safety. Know the territory, especially at night!

It's a big lake

The tides make the ocean behave like a stream. But the ocean is also a very big lake. As you would in a lake, look for structure, drop-offs, and channels. Weed beds hold food and hide predators. Underwater wrecks provide all kinds of hidey-holes.

It's what's underneath that counts

Sometimes, tides or storms will carry big mats of floating weeds and grasses along with them. Bait fish and shellfish are often in and around these mats. Floating weeds and grasses also cut down on light. All of these factors combine to make a spot that may hold a concentration of game fish.

Look at the birdie

If you see a battalion of diving gulls all bunched up together, you can bet there are bait fish underneath them. What happens is this: Game fish encircle the bait fish and force them to the surface; and then, while the bait fish are penned up, the gulls have easy pickings. My advice is this: Follow the birds. My other advice: Follow the bird (as in one bird). Sometimes, a lone bird diving repeatedly in the same place indicates that a feeding striper or a cruising sailfish is nearby. Check it out.

TIP

Don't trust terns. Terns are little birds, very much like swallows. You will see them dipping and diving along the shore. While diving gulls are a pretty sure bet as a sign of game fish, terns are a 50-50 shot. If you get under a flock of terns and cast a few times but catch nothing, move on. All that commotion means that the terns have found food but the game fish haven't.

Temperature counts, too

Fish when the water is at the right temperature and you will catch fish. Fish when the water is the wrong temperature and you will catch nothing. It's that simple. As in freshwater fishing, a thermometer (or a more-sophisticated electronic monitor) is one of the most practical angling aids you can buy. As noted in Chapters 1 and 2, all fish have an optimum temperature range. Seek it out.

When

The quick answer to the question "When do I fish?" is simple: Whenever you get the chance. Most of the time, you can find a way to catch something. You may not be able to fish for the big guys, or you may have to forget about some of the glamour fish and go for panfish, flounder, or whatever. Still, it's fishing. The other thing to remember is this: Game fish don't go to sleep during the day; they just go to different places. Sometimes, they go to deeper water. Sometimes, they visit reefs or nooks in a rocky shore. But they are somewhere, and they can be caught if you know where to go and how to fish. The important thing is to fish whenever you can.

Stars and stripers

At the turn of the century, millions of immigrants' first landfall in America was on Ellis Island, through which nearly 20 million future Americans passed. A causeway connects Ellis Island with the New Jersey shore. About ten years ago, I was fishing there with Captain Joe Shastay, the pioneering fishing guide in New York Harbor. The causeway runs over a shallow flat where you can pick up schoolie stripers (up to 5 pounds). You can use a trout or freshwater bass rig for these guys. We arrived at sunset on December 23, which was a cold but windless winter evening. I rigged up. Joe took the temperature of the water at the end of the outgoing tide. It was cold — about 45°F.

"Water from the mountains upstate," Joe said. "A little cold for bass. Wait 'til the tide turns."

Within the hour, just as Joe had predicted, I began to see feeding fish all around. What happened was, the incoming tide had brought in warmer ocean water (49°F), and the stripers turned on. Fishing under those conditions was like flipping an on/off switch. I cast and caught, cast and caught, and cast and caught (maybe 50 fish). The fishing couldn't have been more productive.

If it is true that the early bird gets the worm, it is also probably true that the early worm gets the fish. (And the late worm, too.) In other words, long experience has shown that dawn and dusk are very productive times. When the world changes over from those animals on night duty to those that come out in the daytime, you have another one of those edges that I spoke about earlier in this chapter. This particular edge is not a physical edge, but an edge in time. The important thing about all edges is that they are transition zones, and some creatures have a natural advantage in making that transition. The skillful predator exploits that advantage. Just as the trout grows bold and loses caution when many mayflies are on the water, many predators grow bolder in dim light. Maybe, in dim light, the bait fish feel that they are less visible; they get a little cocky, and the game fish know that the pickings will be good. Anglers observe this behavior, and that's when they are on the water.

The best of times

Sometimes, the fish totally ignore the rules and come out to feed when all the books say they have no business being out and about. But of course, if fish didn't make fatal mistakes like that, no one would ever catch them. For most fish, most of the time, here's when you want to be fishing:

- At dawn and dusk.

TIP

- ✏ On cloudy overcast days (which have similar light conditions to dawn and dusk).

- ✏ For trout, fish the pleasant time of the day. Water temperature in spring and fall is usually optimal for insect activity in the warmest part of the day. In the summer, the prime insect time is when things cool down a bit.

- ✏ Apple blossom time. For shad, for trout, for smallmouth bass, and probably for a good many other fish, the locals will tell you, "Don't fish until the dogwood blooms," or "Wait until the redbud leaves are as big as squirrel ears." What these tips all mean is that generations of anglers have noticed that when the spring really starts to put some early flowers and leaves out, it is a sign that the air and water are warming. This is when fish are going to stir from their winter doldrums.

The worst of times

TIP

In my opinion, you can hang it up right after a big barometric swing (though there are some anglers who have exactly the opposite opinion). Time and time again, it has been my experience that a change in the weather means that fish are going to need some time to adjust to the change. A Finnish fisheries biologist (whom I ran into years ago while fishing with the Rapala brothers on one of the lakes near their hometown) said that it was his belief that bait fish don't have sophisticated organs to compensate for pressure. He believed that a falling barometer meant that bait (or at least Finnish bait) had to go deeper to equalize pressure. When the bait fish went deeper into the water, the game fish followed, and anglers who were using top water plugs and dry flies were out of luck. According to his theory, a rising barometer should have the opposite effect and should make for good topwater action, but I have never noticed that effect. If you play the odds, my advice is give the fish a little time to adjust to a change in the weather.

"If you don't fish at night, you won't catch big fish"

If you hang around Montauk Point, you will hear that the hard-core guys (supposedly the guys who catch the big babies) fish in the middle of the night, dressed in wet suits and using miners' lamps for illumination. I can tell you right now that I have seen 50-pound striped bass pulled out of the surf at nine o'clock in the morning under a bright sun. I have seen such striped bass on top of the water, boiling under bait all through clear fall days. It's a great time to fish. So, no, you don't have to fish when it is dark to have a chance to catch big fish.

However . . .

You will catch more fish in low-light conditions than you will catch in the heat of the day. You will catch more fish on cloudy days than you will catch on sunlit ones. You will have a much better chance in shallow water when darkness provides bait fish with the feeling, but not always the reality, of security from predatory game fish.

A Few Tips That Didn't Fit Anywhere Else

Here are a couple of pointers that I want you to remember. All of them have to do with getting your offering to the fish without scaring the fish away. Remember, scared fish don't eat! And if they don't eat, they don't take whatever it is you are throwing at them.

Where do they all go?

I had always wondered where fish go to after their early morning feed. One day I found out. We were fishing for stripers out on Gardiners Bay at the tip of Long Island. Gardiners Bay has a very long, skinny sand bar that was created by the killer hurricane of 1938 that boiled up out of the Gulf Stream, causing hundreds of deaths. We were catching bluefish in very skinny water. We could see their fins waving as they positioned themselves down tide of the bait. The blues were feeding as if they were trout holding below a riffle. Then, when the tide turned, they disappeared. We moved to the other side of the bar, thinking that the blues had changed position.

Our guide, Paul Dixon, picked up his push pole and began moving us parallel to the beach, about a hundred yards out.

We found no feeding activity anywhere along the shore. The surface was calm. But when we reached about four feet of depth — not much depth, but enough relative to the shallows on the shore — I began to see stripers. As Paul poled over them, they darted like a school of minnows. For the next mile and a half, we passed over thousands and thousands of stripers. We even caught a few. So the next time anyone tells you fish disappear after sunrise, remember that all the fish in the world could be just a little further offshore.

Stay calm

You see a fish that is finning quietly just below the surface. (No scene is more enticing to an angler, nor more likely to make a fish feel skittish.) When approaching a fish like this (in fact, when moving through *any* water where you think you might find fish), keep these four simple rules in mind:

Take it slow

The faster you move, the more likely you are to make a disturbance. In really calm water, moving slowly is a matter of taking a step, waiting a second for the waves to subside, and then taking another step. The same goes for rowing your boat or canoe — do it slowly and steadily.

Quiet, please

Be careful about banging your oars, scraping rocks with your boots, or walking with heavy footfalls. Sound really does travel well underwater, and it transfers very well between land (underwater rocks, riverbanks, and beaches) and the water. Take it easy, and if you must do anything, do it quietly.

Stay out of sight

In most cases, if you can see the fish, the fish can see you. This rule is not always true, however. For example, if you are downstream of a rising trout, it will probably not notice you. The basic rule is this: Stay out of the line of sight of wary fish. Here are some tips you can follow to do that:

- **Blend into the background:** Although you don't need full camouflage, wearing clothing that is the same color as the background against which the fish will see you is a good idea. (Remember that fish are not used to seeing fluorescent exercise outfits in their usual environment.)

- **Keep a low profile:** Just like the guy who wants to keep his head on his shoulders while hiding in a foxhole, the angler should stay low and out of sight.

Really — I mean it — be quiet!

I just want to emphasize how important it is to stay cool, calm, collected, and quiet. The more enticing the fish, the harder keeping quiet may be; but the only way that you are going to be sure not to scare off a trophy fish is by being quiet.

Fish near, then far

Everyone likes to cast as far as he or she can. This feat can really impress your friends. The fish, however, couldn't care less. All the fish cares about is this: "Does that thing with a hook attached to it look like food that I want to eat?" If that thing with the hook does look like edible food, you want to make sure that you have done nothing else to put the fish on its guard, so disturb as little water as possible. The best way to tackle a stretch of water is to fish the water that is nearest to you and then fish progressively further with each cast. If you do it the other way round, any fish that is close in is going to have been through a great deal of distracting commotion by the time that you are ready to cast to him.